EVERYONE FROM F
HOMEOWNI
TO RETIRED EMPTY-N
WILL BENEFIT FROM

BRIAN COSTELLO'S

MAKING MONEY
FROM YOUR
MORTGAGE

Let's face it, for most people a mortgage represents the largest long-term investment of their life. With this in mind, Brian Costello, Canada's premier financial consultant, has written a comprehensive and easy-to-use guide on how to get a more profitable mortgage to work for you and your financial future.

Did you know that by entering into a weekly mortgage you can save $51,573 and shave 11 years off a 25 year term? Or that a weekly savings plan can help you chop $100 off your monthly mortgage payments? Or that by putting aside an extra dollar each working day you could save $15,819 on a $40,000 mortgage? Brian Costello will show you how.

After all, why work for your mortgage when it can work for you!

BRIAN COSTELLO

MAKING MONEY

FROM YOUR

MORTGAGE

Random House
Toronto

Originally published in Canada in 1987 by Random House of Canada Limited.

Canadian Cataloguing in Publication Data
Costello, Brian
  Making money from your mortgage

Updated for 1991.
ISBN 0-394-22243-1

1. Mortgages — Canada.   2. Investments — Canada.
I. Title.

HG5159.C86 1991   332.63′244′0971   C91-093390-1

Source for the chart "Homeowners versus renters" on page 16: Clayton Research Associates based on Toronto Real Estate Board, Statistics Canada, CMHC and Bank of Canada data.

Design: Brant Cowie/ArtPlus Limited
Cover Photograph: Karen Blackwell

Printed and bound in Canada

To my wife Kathy and son Brian.

Table of Contents

Introduction

"Your money – that's what mortgages are all about."

There is perhaps nothing so desirable as having a roof over your head. And what a break for us that we have the right to own property – to own the one thing that gives us stability, roots, and a place to grow. Those who rent living space miss out on this, and they end up paying more for it – after all, they get nothing back when they move: the increased property value remains with the property owner, their landlord! In addition, the tenant probably bears over the years any further operating costs through rent increases. The individual who owns rather than rents may pay a higher monthly cost in the early stages before rent increases, but will reap the profits as the value of his or her property rises.

This book has two purposes: one is to help turn the

tables on the lenders – to help borrowers negotiate a better deal on their loans and pay them much faster than normal. The second purpose is to demonstrate the advantages of using that paid-for asset to double, triple, even quadruple your money so that you have not only paid for your residence but also any additional assets that are rising in value at the same time.

Remember, the homeowner uses his money to purchase a residence that provides a roof, protection against inflation, and an eventual return well in excess of the cost of the investment. Even when comparing the purchase price of the house to the selling price, the homeowner triples his or her money *and* has a place to live.

Too many people are content to pay off their mortgages at the lender's pace when, with a little strategy, an asset base can be created that will work in a number of ways to increase their wealth. The most important thing is to pay off non-tax-deductible loans as quickly as possible.

Always leave in mind, your mortgage represents the largest long-term investment in your life. MAKING MONEY FROM YOUR MORTGAGE will help you to also make it the most profitable.

Brian K. Costello

Chapter 1

Tax Reform

Finance Minister Michael Wilson's tax-reform package, it now turns out, was a pretty mixed bag, involving a great deal of giving with one hand and taking back with the other. But whatever the final verdict, one thing it has done for certain (aside from making financial planning more crucial than ever) is to confirm the value of owning a house.

For most Canadians, there is now no better investment vehicle than their principal residence, and they don't have to look hard to see why. For the small-scale investor, the basic rules of the game have changed – in particular, the capital-gains rules. The sliding scale that was to have allowed individuals to accrue up to $500,000 worth of capital gains before having to pay tax has now been capped at the 1987 level of $100,000 – unless you own a farm or shares in a small business corporation. Not only that, but the nonexempt gains will be taxed at a higher rate than before. The tax credit on dividends has been watered down, too, so that they don't appear quite as attractive as before (although I think they're still extremely viable). Third, no longer is the first $1,000 worth of an individual's investment income tax-free; everyone who owns, for example, Canada Savings Bonds, or even a straight savings account in the bank, now has to live with the fact that from penny one, on the first day of 1989, it's taxable.

To the small investor, the message that came through from tax reform, loud and clear, was this: either get out of your interest-bearing investments or rethink how you manage them. And that may necessitate taking a fresh look at your mortgage. Before tax reform, lots of people could sit on their Canada Savings Bonds or their term deposits and say to themselves: "I'm earning 10 per cent on my tax-free income, while my mortgage is costing me 10 per cent a year in interest, so I'm breaking even." That's just not the case any more.

So if you're looking for a modest investment, the new rules mean looking beyond the traditional standbys. Now, with the new capital-gains ceiling, you may think you'll never reach it, and perhaps you won't. But buy a cottage or a piece of rental real estate and resell it a few years down the line; or make a small killing in the stock market; or have your mutual funds pay off, which they probably will. It may not be nearly as difficult as you think to use up that $100,000, especially in a generally buoyant economy. And the upshot is you're left with the one totally tax-free investment that has survived tax reform unscathed: your principal residence. It doesn't matter whether you own a million-dollar mansion or a $50,000 bungalow, the rule still applies: if it's your principal residence and in the event you sell it, the profit – regardless of ANY other circumstances – is tax-free. And that's not true of anything else. Whether you own a frame house in Vancouver or a condo in Saskatoon, a cottage in the Ontario woods or a ski chalet in Alberta, being able to claim that piece of property as your own principal residence makes more economic sense than ever before. We'll examine in detail some of the options available in deciding what is, and what is not, a principal residence because there's more here than you might think.

In a sense, therefore, Mr. Wilson's tax changes have solidified the great Canadian dream of owning your own home, and on that basis I have to congratulate him. But at the same time, what we have to do with these new parameters is use them to our advantage. And there's another new reason for securing a stake in the housing market. In the long term, tax reform will have the direct effect of making property values increase, the reason being that Mr. Wilson has said to real estate companies: "When you borrow to buy large chunks of land, you can no longer claim the interest on the loan as a tax deduction." Under the new rules, instead of being able to claim the cost of vacant or unused land as a writeoff, developers are required to capitalize it, which is to say add it on to the value of the land. When the land developer does eventually sell, his tax bill will be a bit lower, but in the meantime (he'll reason) he's going to have to have more resources to survive. And that means he's going to pass the cost along to the purchaser.

There's been a change in the administration of property taxes as well. Under the new scheme of things, municipalities have to pay their remittances to the federal government more frequently than they did, which will leave less cash in the till. If city council can't earn as much as it used to, because it has less money to invest, there's going to be a shortfall. Guess who's going to have to pick up that shortfall?

For most of us, higher housing costs will translate into bigger mortgages, and taking on a mortgage is the biggest expenditure of our life. As we'll see, a mortgage that's set up, amortized, and paid off in the normal way can be a deadly business. The name of the game, therefore, is to turn things around. So now, more than ever, we need to look at making some or all of the mortgage tax-deductible. We also need to pay it down as fast as possible, plus we have to examine a whole host of other options that will lessen the burden of this debt.

Because – if we so choose – we can then begin to treat this whole thing as an asset instead of a liability. A piece of real estate that steadily grows in value, completely tax-free, becomes a tool, a device that allows the homeowner to approach the bank and say: "Look, I don't have to share the profits on this investment with anybody. This is the best collateral you'll ever see." And armed with that collateral, the individual can borrow the money to buy other assets. These too are tax-free up to the first $100,000, in the case of stocks, mutual funds, or real estate. Sink your teeth into a small business or a farm, and the ceiling is still half a million dollars. And remember something else: capital-gains tax – in any category of investment – never kicks in unless you actually sell the investment.

The feature of Mr. Wilson's reform package that produced the biggest headlines was his assurance that it would lower the overall tax bite for most people. The federal finance department estimated that four households in five would enjoy a cut in taxes in 1988, with the typical family (one earner, two children) ending up $555 ahead. At the same time, however, it's equally clear that a lot of taxpayers wound up as losers, and one of the chief reasons (which we'll examine in detail) is the new limit that was slapped on the amount that could be claimed as a tax deduction under our RRSPs. Mr. Wilson held the maximum annual contribution back to $7,500, for 1988, instead of moving it up to the $9,500 that was called for under the previous arrangement. The new restraints have the effect of stretching out the period of time that it will take for a person to reach the $15,500 ceiling: originally, we were to be able to do this by 1991, but now it's 1995. So for those of us who had intended to use our RRSPs to the maximum, in obtaining writeoffs, we've lost a $2,000 deduction worth anything from $400 to $800 – every year.

So what should a person do with that money, which he otherwise could have put to good use? Tax reform, I suspect, will also have the effect of producing a lot of new backyard swimming pools, and other improvements that make houses more valuable. If you're going to sink money into anything, then an investment that doesn't have to have tax paid on it when it's sold is a pretty good bet.

It's ALWAYS true, of course, that overextending oneself is a major mistake – which is where mortgage management comes in. However, say for the sake of argument that one person buys a $200,000 house, while his friend buys a $100,000 house plus a $100,000 cottage. Now, there might well be all kinds of good reasons why somebody should buy the cottage, but looking at it as a straight investment, see what happens under the new rules. Say 5 or 7 years pass, that everything doubles in value, and both men decide to sell everything. The owner of the big house will make a $200,000 profit and, because it's his principal residence, he won't pay a dime in tax. Nor will the friend, on his principal residence, and he'll make a $100,000 profit. But with the cottage, under Mr. Wilson's new rules, it will be a different story. If that person happens to have used up his capital-gains exemption, then $75,000 worth of the profit will now be taxable. If he's in the top tax bracket, he's going to end up giving Revenue Canada a whopping $35,000. If the person is in the 30-per-cent bracket, his gift to the Treasury will be $22,500.

So there was good news and bad news in the tax-reform package, but the net result, with regard to real estate, is that it costs more to own property and that property is now actually a better investment. All the more reason to play with amortization; all the more reason to try to make a mortgage tax-deductible; all the more reason to take a good hard look at what an RRSP can do for you, and how it can make you your own banker; all the more reason why you might want a weekly mortgage, although there's rather more to that than some people realize. Income-splitting with a mortgage also makes greater sense than ever; and there's definitely all the more reason to pay down the loan as quickly as possible.

And this includes pretty well everyone who has a mortgage. Mr. Wilson has told us that tax reform is beneficial because most people are in a slightly lower bracket than they were before. He scoops a lot of those taxes right back, of course, but, in general, the person who DOESN'T currently put his RRSPs to work, or who isn't affected by capital gains or new dividend rules, will probably be a bit further ahead than he used to be. For that person, tax reform will manifest itself in the shape of a bit more disposable cash. And if it does, what better use for it than to do some damage to the principal on his mortgage? Because as we'll see, even minuscule extra payments can make an amazing difference. And it's the same thing with the money that you used to be able to invest to produce $1,000 worth of tax-free income. Since you can't do that any more, you may be far better off simply paying down the loan, and treating that as an investment – which it is.

Mortgage management is a twofold process: as long as the mortgage is there, you take charge of it, rather than vice versa; and once it's paid off – in part or in whole – then you use that equity. And that's the reason, in my opinion, why these days it's imperative that you own the biggest house you can. Why? Because of what we started out by discussing: the new importance attached to the principal-residence capital-gains exemption. It doesn't take a mathematician to see that the net (tax-free) gain of buying, then selling, a $200,000 house will be twice that of the $100,000 home. But a 10-per-cent profit ($20,000 versus $10,000) will actually end up producing a wider spread than that because of the effect of compounding. Good markets and bad markets all have their bearing, but, in the long term, history will show that almost all property rises in value.

So it's a shame to have all that equity built up and not put it to use. But that's not to say an investment has to have a spectacular yield. You can make a good case for a stock or piece of real estate that grows in value, but only produces a modest annual income. Or no income at all – such as the four walls around you.

I'm not suggesting for a moment that the cottage market is about to be driven into oblivion – quite the reverse. And it's true that in many cases the small-scale investor will decide that he'll use up his exemption first and worry about future investments later. Nonetheless, one of the effects of tax reform, in shoring up the principal residence as a tax-free capital gain, is to have given a boost to the renovations industry – and, in turn, the lending industry. The better condition a house is in, the more attractive it is as a piece of collateral. And in the meantime, the fact that there will be no capital-gains tax payable, in the event of the homeowner selling, is not going to be lost on the lender either, who is not stupid. It's simple: the house is now that much more secure as a piece of collateral.

Before tax reform, we could count on half a million dollars' worth of tax-free capital gains and, insofar as most people could safely expect to never reach that limit, that made for all kinds of flexibility in buying stocks, bonds, mutual funds, the condo in Florida – whatever. But it's going to be a lot easier to reach the new $100,000 ceiling than you might think, particularly if the person is putting to work one of the premises of this book, namely using the equity in his or her home as a lever for investment. With a principal residence, however, you can earn millions tax-free, and that's why – in my opinion – the lure of the second home, the weekend cottage, is going to lose some of its luster because, in the event you sell off that cottage, the profit will be subject to tax in a way that didn't used to be the case. By installing a sauna or a jacuzzi in a principal residence, however, the money invested is effectively going to be tax-free. And looking ahead, I can see that it's going to be tempting for some people to sell off their second home entirely, and invest the profit in a bigger family house.

In light of the new importance attached to a home being a principal residence, it makes more sense than ever to think creatively in terms of moving property between different members of the family. If you do own a cottage, for instance – a second home – and you find yourself in a situation wherein either a) you've used up your own capital-gains exemption or b) you don't want to, then you might want to consider passing it along to your son or daughter for a few years. And the reason for this is that by shifting it into another party's name, it becomes his or her principal residence – and therefore tax-free at such time as they sell or give it back to you. I should point out that even if you do actually give it, rather than sell it, there's an extremely good chance Revenue Canada will treat the transaction as a sale, assess it at market value, and either reduce your capital-gains exemption or make you actually pay capital-gains tax, depending on your current status. However, once that's been done, the cottage can now appreciate in value in the name of your son or daughter (it doesn't have to actually be a relative, of course, although that's the simplest route to take) and when it comes back to you, a few years down the road, you will have effectively escaped some of the capital-gains burden. Maybe you want to keep the place in the family anyway because, as well as being an investment, it also provides a lot of pleasure. But the point here is, if you part with it now, the increase in capital gains is going to be significantly less than it would be 10 years or so later on. And if and when the child decides to sell it back to you at that later date, then the increase in value will be part of their tax-free capital gain because it's a principal residence that's been sold. Needless to say, you may not want to have an arrangement whereby you have use of the property for as long as you live. This is just a version of the classic estate freeze that sophisticated planners have always been aware of, but it's going to make more sense than ever because of tax reform. If there's a mortgage on the property, of course, one factor you'll have to look at is which member of the family will take care of it.

For the person who doesn't have a son or daughter, another variation we'll look at in detail a little later on is the estate freeze in reverse: giving the property to an older relative who lives in a rented apartment, or even a retirement home for that matter. Now it may be that at 85, Granny doesn't do a lot of water-skiing anymore – so all the more reason why you should have access to the place – but is there any reason why she shouldn't own it, and then will it back to you when she passes away? As I say, there's always the possibility that any sharp tax planning can be construed as a dodge by Revenue Canada and, indeed, Mr. Wilson included a number of new anti-avoidance rules in his reform bill. It might be tempting to give Granny the cottage for nothing, for example, but the trouble is the taxman, if he wants, can assess it at its market value and say: "You bought it for $20,000 and sold it for $50,000, so there's a $30,000 capital gain." Indeed there is, and there's not much you can do about that. However, it's the gain BEYOND $30,000 that we're interested in here. Because don't forget that it may be years, or decades, before the property comes back to you. In the unhappy event that Granny were to die soon after acquiring the cottage, there won't in any case be any appreciable increase in value. But if that property, worth $50,000 at the time she gets it, grows in value to the tune of $70,000 by the time she dies, then that's $20,000 worth of capital-gains deduction, or capital-gains tax, that you'll have escaped. It means that you could then turn around and sell it for $70,000, if you wished, and not pay a nickel in tax because the gift from Granny hasn't gone up in value at all. If it's gone up by $5,000, then that represents your capital gain. Since Granny's estate will have to declare its capital gain at the time the cottage is bequeathed to you, then her capital-gains status has to be taken into account all along. However, it's far from unusual to find an older person who hasn't used up his or her exemption and, where this applies, a few simple moves, accompanied by suitable goodwill all around, can save you a lot of money.

If you already have a good-sized chunk of equity in your home, then Mr. Wilson's new rules also make the practice of using that equity to buy shares in a small business - a small, closely held corporation - more viable than ever because, here, the first $500,000 worth of capital gains is still tax-free. This type of business is very often a family operation and it's a great place to allow assets to compound tax-free. Take note, however, that there's a new requirement that you own those shares, or that corporation, for 2 years or more.

Income-splitting is not the game that it used to be. No longer can you simply give money to a spouse, or lend it to her/him at a bargain-basement interest rate. These days, if you lend money to your wife/husband you must, by law, charge what's called the prescribed interest rate; the government sets it every quarter and bases it on the yield of Treasury Bills. However, with a principal residence, the property law of Canada states that a house is half owned by you and half owned by your spouse - regardless of who actually paid for it. This means that in the event you sell it, you can take the profit and split it down the middle, 50-50, as you would in the event you got divorced. More on that later.

Recognizing the $100,000 capital-gains limit, it's also become more valuable than ever to put investment property in the name of your children. Agreed, it's a move that's pretty hard to justify in the case of a minor (however shrewd he/she may have been with his Baby Bonus cheques), but when they reach 18, this is something that bears a good deal of scrutiny. If you have $50,000 worth of investments every penny of the interest on that is exposed to tax. If you make $5,000 worth of interest on that money, then a person in the 40-per-cent tax bracket is going to part with $2,000 by the time he's finished. So why not, instead, take that $50,000 and use it as the down payment on a rental property in your child's name? If, rather than investments per se, you have equity built up in your house, you can always create collateral by transferring to the child the right to the use of the house. You, of course, would retain control of the investment (since you might not want your son to sink all your equity in Acme Buggy Whips), but in the meantime, he's been given a great grubstake, the interest on which is tax-deductible. It could be any kind of investment, but the advantage to rental real estate, as a business operation, is that it allows the child to hold on to it, and have access to it, while it grows in value. He might not sell it for 50 years, in which case he doesn't have to think about capital-gains taxes for 50 years, and Canada is full of people who own rental properties that they never sell. Instead, they use them as collateral to launch other ventures, and it's a strategy that makes all kind of sense. And as soon as the rental property has acquired enough equity of its own, then you, the parent, can take the lien off your own house, and the child can begin to make his own way. I'm really a fan of this strategy, because it allows me, the parent, to use the assets that I've built up to get my children started. An offshoot of that ploy is buying a rental property for a child in a college town, an option we'll examine later on, because here, too, the rules have altered under tax reform, and created new opportunities.

As we've noted, one of the planks of tax reform was that interest on business loans, while still fully deductible, now gets carried forward, in the same way that depreciation on a property always has been, and is applied against the capital-gains exemption in the event that the investment is sold. For this reason, and taking into account the fact that the exemption itself has been reduced sharply, I think we have seen a change in investment thinking. Because while it makes as much sense as ever to use equity in a piece of property to invest, it now makes a lot more sense to hold on to that investment and NOT sell, and instead let the investment grow, which in turn becomes a lever for new ventures. In sum, the name of the game for many smaller investors will lie in NOT triggering capital gains. Once the $100,000 mark has been reached, on the other hand, the interest on business loans is completely tax-deductible, as before – it can't be carried forward to balance against the exemption because there isn't any exemption – so at that point, it will make more sense to write it off and pay capital-gains tax.

The new importance of being able to claim a piece of property as a primary residence will compel some individuals, who perhaps rent an apartment in the city, to think in terms of buying a country cottage – because, remember, it doesn't matter how many weeks of the year you live there; as long as it's the ONLY house you own, and as long as it's not rented out for most of the year, it still qualifies as a principal residence. But at the same time, a number of individuals may decide to hold on to country homes rather than sell them and thereby be subject to the new capital-gains rules. In the long term, this will likely have a bearing on prices. So taking these 2 factors together, if you are thinking of buying, there's probably no time like the present.

With property, as with anything else, the great mistake lies in getting in over your head. But assuming that a person is able to carry the cost of a house, the only individual I would counsel against owning real estate is someone who's unable to look after it, perhaps because he or she is too old, or infirm – and a house DOES have to be taken care of. This brings up the topic of condominiums because, as countless retired people have realized, when the time comes, there's a lot of sense in disposing of a large property, buying a smaller one, and sinking the difference into an investment that will pay for the monthly maintenance on a condo. Which is not to say everything about condominiums is sweetness and light. When they first appeared on the scene, they were designed as a form of low-cost house, and if that's the way a prospective buyer looks at them, he could be making a mistake, in terms of an investment. Why? Because even a modest single-family home will 9 times out of 10 outpace a multi-family unit, such as a condo. With expensive, well-located condominiums with well-heeled occupants who've bought a condo not because it was the cheapest housing they could find, but because they simply don't have the time to look after a house, it tends to be a different story. So we see here the same principle at work that we mentioned at the start of this chapter: the more you can spend the better. Because in the end, a cheap house remains just that: a cheap house. One drawback to the condo, whatever its price range, is that there are overheads that the owner has no control over. He might think that the lobby really doesn't need to be refurbished, or that the underground parking is just fine the way it is. The trouble is he only has one vote. To me, that's another argument for the single-family home.

Either way, however, the evidence in favor of owning SOME type of property, as opposed to renting and investing savings elsewhere, is pretty compelling. A recent study of Metropolitan Toronto, over the 15-year period between 1971 and 1986 (p. 16), compared the increase in value of the average house over that time span with an individual who decided to rent a 3-bedroom apartment and invest the equivalent of the buyer's down payment and closing costs ($7,003 in all) in a Guaranteed Income Certificate, with an annual average return of 7.72 per cent. The average price for a Toronto home, back in those halcyon days, was $32,513. With 20 per cent down ($6,503) and a starting 5-year mortgage at 9 1/2 per cent, subsequently renewed at the going rate, the homeowner would have spent just over $51,000 on his mortgage by 1986; property taxes would have totalled $13,392; and there would still be almost $20,000 owing on the mortgage. That illustrates what a killer the amortization process can be (a topic we'll put under the magnifying glass later on), but at the same time, the owner could take comfort in the fact that his house by that time would have risen to a whopping $139,000 in value. His friend the renter, on the other hand, would have given an average of $72,745 to his landlord, over the years, while earning about $26,600 on his GIC. And the upshot of the whole thing is that after those 15 years had passed, the person who took a deep breath and bought the house – for what undoubtedly seemed like a great deal of money at the time – was nearly $100,000 ahead of his counterpart. And don't forget that in all those years, the renter was paying no tax on the first $1,000 of his GIC yield, an exemption that's now in the history books, thanks to Mr. Wilson.

All investments, in a sense, involve peaks and valleys, and the key thing in investing in property – as opposed to speculating, which is a different ball of wax – is being prepared to stick things out long enough to weather any of the storms that can – and will – appear. The most dramatic fall in property values we've seen in recent years took place in Alberta, on the coattails of the energy boom/bust, and further fueled by record interest rates.

Homeowners versus renters

Owner Option	1971-1986
1. Average MLS dwelling price at start of period	$ 32,513
2. Outlays:	
a) Down payment (20%)	$ 6,503
b) Closing costs	500
c) Total required savings	7,003
3. Amount of mortgage (#1 minus #2)	$ 26,010
4. Five-year mortgage rate at start of period	9.43%
5. Total mortgage payments for period	$ 51,129
6. Total property taxes for period	$ 13,392
7. Total PIT (#5 plus #6)	$ 64,521
8. Mortgage principal remaining at end of period	$ 19,960
9. Average MLS dwelling price at end of period	$138,925
10. Equity at end of period (#9 minus #8)	$118,965
11. Less original outlay (#2c)	$ 7,003
12. Gain (#10 minus #11)	$111,962

Renter Option	
13. Original investment (#2)	$ 7,003
14. Five-year GIC rate at start of period	7.72%
15. Return on original investment	$ 26,618
16. Total rent payments	$ 72,745
17. Cumulative difference between owner PIT and total rent payments (#7 minus#16)	($ 8,224)
18. Interest on investment of above cumulative difference	($ 5,562)
19. Total of return on original investment plus cumulative difference in annual payments (including interest) (#15 plus #17 plus #18)	$ 12,832

Comparison	
20. Owner gain (#12)	$111,962
21. Renter returns plus housing cost difference (#19)	$ 12,832
22. Difference (#20 minus #21)	$ 99,130

For those who HAD to sell in those circumstances, such as workers whose livelihood had depended on the oil patch, and who now had to move on, the whole cycle was pretty bad news. But a cycle is exactly that – and the individuals who could hang on eventually saw prices come back up again. The average Canadian moves home every 3 years and, for most people, in my view, that's really the minimum period they should be looking at in terms of being able to ride out the bumps in the marketplace. And the longer she does stay put, the more equity she'll have in her home and the more ways of being able to put this asset to work for her, instead of the other way around.

We've sung the praises of investing in a principal residence, because it's tax-free in a way that nothing else is, but how should a person approach this? It's been proven that some additions/renovations produce better growth than others, so what should you be looking at? That really depends on why you're investing because a key distinction to bear in mind is the difference between making a house more VALUABLE and making it more SALABLE, which are horses of a different color. And as far as investment goes, you should be thinking of both.

We've mentioned swimming pools. Right now, it's generally recognized that it takes about 10 years to recoup the $10,000 or so that it takes to install a pool, the reason being that it depreciates – it's made of bricks and mortar – and so if you think you're to make money instantly by putting one in, chances are you're wrong. Of course, a swimming pool is there for enjoyment, and for the person who does what we've suggested she might do, and consolidate 2 homes into one bigger one, a pool might be the first thing she thinks of. But even though the pool business is probably going to leapfrog, if you're putting one in as an inducement to a buyer, you might do well to consider some other options because not everybody wants a swimming pool in his backyard, for all sorts of reasons. And a great place to spend the afternoon is not the same thing as a great investment.

A driveway is a much safer bet, especially in an urban area, and so is a garage, which is better yet. It sounds boring – until you try to find a parking spot in some downtown neighborhoods. At that point, you'll find that a parking spot on what used to be the front lawn can be worth its weight in gold when weighed against the hassles of permit-parking and having to walk blocks to get to your car. Gardens and landscaping I'd put a lot further down the list. Inside the house, the item that SHOULD be remodeled, second to none, is the kitchen, which is where half the buying public head straight off. Lots of cupboard space, light color, lots of light. But don't bother installing too many expensive appliances because people frequently have their own. Studies have shown that a sundeck off the family room with sliding doors almost invariably recaptures more than it costs to install, as well as being a big selling feature; fresh air is more popular than ever. So too with a main floor bathroom, which both older people and mothers with small children are always keen on – no stairs to fall down. A heat-efficient fireplace is a good investment; likewise a basement family room – as long as the ceilings aren't too low because, if they are, the construction costs of changing that can be prohibitive. In-built vacuuming systems tend to be a throwaway, and central air conditioning is another item that doesn't always recapture its cost (unless you happen to be selling during a heat wave, in which case it can be a real plus).

As with all these items, and bearing in mind that we're looking at them in terms of their INVESTMENT, the key question has to be the amount of use they get. When you're selling a house, you have to put on blinkers – look at it as though you've never seen it before, and then decide whether the driveway should be recoated and the front windows repainted. My experience has been that a major painting job on the whole house doesn't pay off, but a touch-up job works wonders. Upstairs, the biggest selling feature, by far, and one that always recoups its cost, is an en suite bathroom in the master bedroom, which allows for privacy from children/guests. Skylights are becoming popular, but forget about putting in drapes. As far as structural changes go, it almost always pays to turn a 2-bedroom home into a 3-bedroom one, but that's not necessarily the case with adding a fourth bedroom. What we're talking about here are the sure things. Include in that category renovations that create a rental unit; and an upper floor apartment tends to be a better bet than a remodeled basement.

We've drawn the distinction between a house's value and its salability, and those are just a few ideas that will enhance both. Now, it may well be that you don't have the least desire to sell your house, its tax-free status not-withstanding. Instead, perhaps, you want to use it as the asset that it is and borrow against it. Either way, money invested in improvements makes sense because the more valuable the property, the better the collateral it becomes. Like no change in recent history, tax reform has affirmed the wisdom of owning property. But some of the topics we've touched on so far may not be applicable in the early years.

In taking aim at a number of sophisticated tax shelters, either wiping them out altogether or watering them down, Mr. Wilson has made investment in good-quality stocks, or real estate, a no-contest winner. There had been widespread fear that interest on investment loans would no longer be tax-deductible. Happily, however, these fears proved unfounded, and one of the most valuable devices for the homeowner with equity in his house has been left in place. Because of a recent case that came before the Supreme Court, which we'll examine, one of the ploys that we've always used, namely making a mortgage tax-deductible, is going to have to be approached in a slightly different way than in the past. Nonetheless, it's still the case that the more equity you can pull out of your house, the more options you have in using that security to under-pin various investment strategies.

But that's at one end of the scale – the end occupied by the person who's paid off a good portion of his mortgage. Down toward the other end, however, in the earlier years, it's often the case that all the homeowner can see is a mountain of debt – a massive liability that has to be paid with after-tax dollars – and not a glimpse of tax relief on the horizon.

Well, it just doesn't have to be like that.

Chapter 2

A Tax-Deductible Mortgage

A mortgage, let's face it, is a tool with which the borrower can be gouged. If it's amortized over 25 years and paid off in the usual way, it will generally have cost at least three times its face value by the time the last payment has been made. And don't forget it's being paid for with dollars that have already been taxed. If you're in the 40-per-cent income-tax bracket and you have a mortage that's running at 10 per cent, then by the time you make that payment each month, you've had to earn the equivalent of about 17 per cent to do so; if you're in the 50-per-cent bracket, you've had to earn double the amount. Hence the cardinal rule that says: pay off your mortgage as fast as you possibly can because as a mortgage it's not normally tax-deductible.

I say normally because the point is that it can be. One of the features of the Wilson tax program was to replace deductions with tax credits. But in this case, when we say "deductions," we still mean just that: money that is removed from an individual's gross income before the tax bite. And the fact is you don't have to be an accountant to develop a strategy that will a) make all or part of the mortgage tax-deductible; and b) by doing that, also accelerate the prepayment schedule. Yet it's amazing how many Canadians write out a mortgage cheque every month without realizing this. The philosophy – as well as the rules – about taxation in Canada were central to Mr. Wilson's reform package. Noting that, in 1983, 110,000 of Canada's 320,000 profitable companies paid no income tax at all, his white paper made it clear that tax avoidance, per se, is under new scrutiny, and specifies that "the reduction, avoidance, deferral or refund of tax" is not, in itself, a bona fide business practice. That's his way of looking at things. On the other hand, there is a long-standing and completely respectable school of thought that says that minimizing the government's share is part of what taxation is all about. So take your choice. I'm not saying Revenue Canada – or the banking industry – are necessarily going to be as happy as you are about some of these ideas because you may end up costing them both a big chunk of cash. On the other hand, whose cash is it?

One thing that didn't change with Mr. Wilson's reforms is the wording of the The Income Tax Act of Canada, which says that a taxpayer can deduct from his/her taxable income "all interest paid on money which was borrowed for the purpose of earning income." So what we're talking about here is investments. And because a Canadian mortgage is not normally regarded as an investment, the way to make it so essentially involves taking money that's tied up elsewhere, paying down part of the principal, and then borrowing back that cash to buy something on which the interest for the loan IS deductible.

What you choose to invest in is up to you. It can be anything from real estate to a business venture to shares in a mutual fund. A farmer can take out a tax-deductible loan to buy seed or fertilizer; a musician can write off the cost of the borrowing to buy new equipment. Up until 1981, another way for the homeowner to do things was to pay down the mortgage with savings, then borrow again to invest in an RRSP, with the interest on the loan being tax-deductible. However, that's history, and the basic criterion now is that there has to be some benefit to the economy taking place – cash piling up in the bank is not considered eligible. If you make a move that will enable you, indirectly, to write off the interest on a mortgage, it does have to involve a legitimate investment.

Here's how it works. A scenario might be that you have a $150,000 mortgage on your house and $50,000 sunk into secure nondeductible bank accounts of one type or another – a term deposit, Guaranteed Investment Certificates, Canada Savings Bonds, or perhaps an education fund for your child. Say both the mortgage and the savings carry at a 10-per-cent interest rate. The savings, none of which are tax-deductible, are generating $5,000 a year, and because you're in the 40-per-cent tax bracket, you lose $2,000 of that and keep $3,000. The interest on the mortgage, meanwhile, involves 12 monthly payments of $1,341.73 – $16,100.82 a year, $15,000 of which is straight interest, nondeductible, and all of which disappears forever.

The mortgage comes due, it's time to refinance, and the cost of borrowing is still 10 per cent. Consider what would happen if you now cashed in that $50,000 worth of investments, paid down the mortgage to $100,000 and then – even right there at the lender's desk – immediately borrowed the $50,000 back to buy something on which the interest is tax-deductible. As we'll see in a moment, that "something" might have to be different from the investment you've just cashed in, but let's just say you decide to buy a mutual fund. Two things will now have changed. First, in your 40-per-cent tax bracket, the real price tag of the $5,000 annual cost of the loan has dropped to $3,000, meaning that the money that would otherwise have disappeared is now working on your behalf. Second, the mutual fund has started producing a yield that, as long as it stays inside the plan, is tax-free.

Revenue Canada's rationale for letting you do this is that by investing you're creating wealth. And, of course, it has conditions attached. One, the money must – outright – be invested, and two, the investment must produce some sort of a regular income. But that doesn't mean it has to be a winning income. As most people in business know, it's quite acceptable to borrow, invest, and lose money, provided there is the expectation of an eventual profit. But the proposition has to be reasonable and there has to be actual business taking place; raw land and gold mines, for instance, are two investment ventures that are not considered acceptable for the purpose of making a loan tax-deductible.

And neither is anything that could be construed as a sham. It used to be that, in the above situation, a person could simply sell off his investments, pay down the mortgage, and then immediately buy back those very same investments and write off the cost of the loan. I've done this myself and very likely there are still people doing so, and getting away with it. However, a word of caution. There was a landmark case that came before the Supreme Court of Canada in April 1987, and the judge, in his ruling, opened something of a can of worms. The case involved the Bronfman brothers and a trust they'd set up on behalf of a niece, whereby at intervals money was paid out to her. Essentially, what the Bronfmans were doing was borrowing new money to make the payments, then writing off the interest on the loan. In its ruling, which went against the Bronfmans, the court outlined a "sham" concept that will likely be persuasive in other Canadian courts in years to come. We'll see. Now, the judge didn't specifically address the question of mortgages, but he did say that it appeared to him there could be a sham in the case of the person who sells his investments, buys a principal residence, then immediately borrows against that piece of property. The individual who sells investments to buy a house, or part of a house, has nothing to be concerned about – he's simply made a smart move. But a direct criss-crossing of cheques could – and I say "could" because the ball is still in the air – be treated as a device for trying to get around the Income Tax Act. There was widespread speculation that Mr. Wilson would directly address this question in his tax-reform paper, but he didn't, and it remains a grey area.

So where does this leave things? It means that what will be at issue in subsequent court cases, if they arise, will be the timing, frequency, and amount of the borrowing. More important, however, will be the nature of the investment itself, and for homeowners who choose to make their mortgage tax-deductible like this, and who want to be 100 per cent certain Revenue Canada is not going to blow the whistle, the key thing will be to put some distance between the investment they've sold off and the one they're buying with the borrowed money.

One way of doing this is simply to make a different investment: if you have stock in Bell Canada, sell it, pay down the mortgage, then borrow again to buy shares in Thomson, or Abitibi-Price. Revenue Canada, or anyone else, would be extremely hard put to show that to be a sham. The other way is to buy back the same investment – perhaps there's only one thing in the world you want to invest in – but to first let some time elapse. If you want to play things really cautiously, you could do both, but either way, the result is a tax-deductible mortgage.

The savings involved can be very large, and the earlier on in the mortgage you make a move, the bigger they'll be because it's only the interest on the loan that's getting written off, as I'll explain in a moment. Equally, however, it should be clear at the outset that this sort of footwork is not for everybody: if you have no savings and a mortgage that's almost equal to the appraised value of the house, there's little chance of being able to make a mortgage tax-deductible because the key to the whole thing is investment. But the person who has both a mortgage and some savings tucked away somewhere, whether in Savings Bonds, term deposits, or GICs, is in a very good position to make this work, and with much smaller sums of money than in our example.

Note that the homeowner is putting his strategy to work at the time when his mortgage has come due, when — as with all mortgages — it's automatically opened up for prepayment. Doing this in mid-term is a different story. Some mortgages are completely closed and can't be paid down at all until the renewal date, but most allow an annual maximum of 10 per cent of the principal to be repaid without penalty. In the case of someone wanting to pay down more than that, the net benefit should be weighed against the rate-differential or 3-month penalty clause that generally applies. In the case of our $150,000 mortgage at 10 per cent, the cost of breaking it would be almost $4,000. So it may well be worth waiting until the term of the mortgage has expired.

But whatever the timing, you can generally be sure the lender will go along with your plans. In the above case, he's now discovered you have $50,000 that you are willing to commit to his collateral. By paying down the mortgage your equity has gone up and that makes you a better risk. Added to that is the fact that the government is effectively paying part of the interest on the loan, which represents further security. And, meanwhile, the investment which you have bought with the loan is growing, tax-free, as long as the money stays where it is. And if you cash it in, triggering capital gains, it will be tax-free too, providing you're within the limits.

The beauty of this is in its simplicity, but you do have to explain very clearly what you're doing. It may be that there are some extra fees asked, a discharge fee, or possibly an appraisal fee. If there are, consider going somewhere else. When a borrower breaks a mortgage, it's usually because he wants to refinance at a lower rate. But in our case, one option for the borrower who wants to open up the mortgage, but who is faced with the 3-month penalty clause, is to offer to reassume the mortgage at the EXISTING rate. Make it clear to the lender that all you want to do is make the thing tax-deductible, and there's every reason why he should be agreeable to that. There's no way, of course, that any lender in his right mind will let you break the mortgage without a penalty AND give it back to you at a lower rate.

So you borrow, you buy your investments, and $50,000 of your mortgage has become tax-deductible. But you have to remember that it's only the interest that is, in effect, being written off. Unless you refinance with a straight demand loan, the monthly payment on the new mortgage is divided into interest, principal, and property taxes. And in the case of the person whose house is used solely as a residence (i.e., there are no additional writeoffs through operating, say, a part-time business in the base-ment), none of these deductions can be made to apply against either taxes or principal. The interest, however, is far and away the bulk of the payment, especially in the early years, which is when you want to do this.

Now, it may be that you don't actually have any sav-ings, perhaps because you've sunk every penny you own into the house. But what if that house on which you owe $100,000 is in fact worth $150,000, through the combina-tion of the down payment, the improvements that have been made, and the general rise in property values? A homeowner can use that increased equity to borrow for the purposes of investment in the same way that he can borrow to buy anything else. And again, borrowing to in-vest in stocks makes him a much more desirable client than his neighbor down the street who's borrowing against his house because he wants a holiday and a new car.

There are four main categories of investment to look at: a business venture, real estate – which we'll examine in detail in the next chapter – stocks, and mutual funds.

Stocks

Stocks don't necessarily pay anything near the yield that the loan is costing you, but since there's always the pros-pect of higher stock prices, the rules of the game are that you're allowed to sustain a loss for some years while claiming the interest on the loan as tax-deductible. And here's an example of how the whole arrangement translates into cash. You've borrowed that $50,000 at 10 per cent – an annual cost of $5,000 – and you're in the 40-per-cent tax bracket, with a gross income of $45,000 a year. Normally, you'd be shelling out $18,000 a year in income tax. But deduct the $5,000 from your taxable income and Revenue Canada's take then drops to a maximum of $16,000. So now, in effect, it's costing you $3,000 to service that loan. Meanwhile, the $50,000 has been invested in stocks with, say, an annual yield of 9.5 per cent, producing an annual income of $4,750. Very few people will earn that profit completely tax-free, but – thanks to the dividend tax credit – most of it will be. If our investor had to part with $250 worth of tax on his dividend, the net result of the whole arrangement would be $1,500 in his pocket.

And the smartest thing he could do with that cash is to make another payment against the mortgage principal. Take another example in which your means are more modest. Say your earnings put you in the 35-per-cent tax bracket, the mortgage is only $40,000, running at 14 per cent, and you've borrowed a tax-deductible $5,000. You invest that $5,000 in stocks, but their value takes a tumble, producing no yield at all. Too bad, but, all the same, the interest cost on the loan will knock about $675 off your taxable income, giving you $236 that you wouldn't otherwise have. And if you took that modest $236 and paid down the mortgage, you'd wipe out about a full year's payments every time you did it – saving you tens of thousands of dollars over the life of the mortgage.

Mutual Funds

More popular than common stocks are mutual funds, and

the chief reason for this is their impressive track record, which allows investors to create a tax deduction as well as manufacture tax-free income – the best of both worlds. As well, the mutual fund is the investment option that's easiest to handle.

A mutual fund can be a group of people investing in widgets, a racehorse, treasury bills, or Canada Savings Bonds. It's simply a pooling of resources for investment purposes, with set parameters. A publicly traded mutual fund will define these in the form of a prospectus, and this is the type of mutual fund that most people like because they don't have to worry about managing it. If I buy a piece of real estate and rent it out, I'm open to being phoned at 2:00 a.m. and told the toilet's overflowing. But one of the things that comes with a mutual fund is the portfolio manager, who is paid to handle that pool of money.

As well as having virtually no work attached to it, the mutual is generally worry-free. Its past performance can be checked in a few minutes and the annual yield is almost certain to have been better than that of a savings account in the bank. But when you're looking at that track record, you should go back at least 10 years for an indicator – long enough to show you not just the good years, but the bad and the ugly ones, too. A fund that's been trading through the 60s, the 70s, and the 80s will have a sufficient spread of profits to let you know what kind of a risk it represents. And for the most part that risk is small. There's only been one example of a mutual fund going bad in recent times, and that one was a fraud.

The interest on the loan used to buy stocks and mutual funds is tax-deductible. But, in addition, any dividends qualify for the dividend tax credit. The rules have changed somewhat under tax reform; it used to be the case that you could automatically make up to a $25,000 profit and pay no tax on that money. That's now been watered down a little, but not too much, and the credit is still powerful enough to offset most of the tax on dividends. Finally, there's the expectation of a capital gain, when the stock rises in value. And when it does – even where the $100,000 ceiling is passed – that too is tax-free as long as the money stays invested in the fund.

This is the reason there's been so much movement into the mutual funds market lately. You don't get all these benefits when you borrow to buy a rental property, for the simple reason that by its very nature that building produces a monthly income. And while you have tax deductions, in the shape of maintenance, heat, hydro, property taxes, advertising for tenants, etc., those expenses may not offset the income.

Every good idea has its pitfalls, and number one in the case of borrowing to invest can be your ability to sleep at night. If you're looking at a loan situation you KNOW you'll be uncomfortable with, don't do it. Secondly, any investment can fail, costing you all the equity in your home. So only go into secure investments. I know people who've borrowed against their homes to invest in a junior gold mine and made a fortune, and I know others who are still paying off the loan although there's no investment left.

There are other traps. Sometimes people go into an investment on what's called a margin loan, from a stockbroker. In this case, the margin loan is automatically adjusted if the prices fall. Say you borrowed $10,000 to buy some stock. You give the broker $10,000, he puts up the same amount, and you buy $20,000 worth of stock. The rules require that you must always have 50-per-cent equity in there. So if the investment falls in value by half, it's worth $10,000 – and now the broker wants his $10,000. You have to put up 5 of it. You get what's termed a margin call, which changes day to day, and, if you don't have the resources to pay it, he'll sell the stock out from underneath you.

But the fact is most people who've become rich have done it with other people's money. If you're an employer and you don't hire anybody, the only work will be what you do yourself. It's the same principle: people go to work, money goes to work. If you can borrow at 12 per cent and use it to earn 20, you're making 8 per cent that is effectively infinite – because you never put up any money in the first place.

When Mr. Wilson brought in tax-free capital gains in 1985, Revenue Canada was effectively taking the sting on both ends: allowing the investor to claim the interest on the loan as a tax deduction because he was using the money to generate investment income, and also permitting a capital-gains holiday. This is something that has changed. It used to be the case that you could write off the loan every year, sell the property at a profit, and until you made $500,000, over the course of a lifetime, pay no tax: a capital gain, followed by an exemption. Two things are now different. First, the cutoff point has been slashed back to $100,000, for most people – after that, they'll be paying income tax on their gains – and, second, the rules about writing off the cost of the loan, vis à vis capital gains, have been altered.

Under tax reform we can still write off the interest on the loan each year. However, any investment expenses that exceed investment income and as a result are deducted against salary and other non-investment income must be accumulated and recaptured later. If for example, you borrowed $100,000 at 12% to finance the cost of buying a rental unit, that loan will create $12,000 in tax write-offs a year. If you had no rental income and were in the 30% tax bracket you would save $3,600 in taxes on other income. Let's say that two years down the road you sell the unit for a $40,000 capital gain. Under the old rules that gain would have been completely free of tax provided you had not yet used your full $100,000 tax-free capital gain deduction. Under the new rules though you must claim the first $24,000 as taxable as Ottawa has allowed you to accumulate that much in tax deductions against other than investment income.

Now in this example we have assumed that you have had no rental income. In real life you would have. In fact, you probably will also earn some interest income and maybe some dividends from stock or mutual funds. It's only the net investment loss that must be accumulated and carried forward. As a result, it is more advantageous to borrow to buy investments like real estate that produce several forms of income. In addition, once you have claimed your $100,000 in capital gains you no longer have to worry about your cumulative net investment losses. All the more reason to earn tax-free capital gains as fast as you can. The arrangement these days is essentially the same as with using depreciation as a tax-saving device, a topic we'll examine in the next chapter, but it remains, nonetheless, an immensely useful one. Although it's no longer true that you can borrow to produce tax-free interest income (that $1,000 worth of tax-free money every year is going to be missed), you can still write off the interest on the loan for as many years as you want, until you trigger a capital gain.

We'll look at the new capital-gains rules more closely because the figures have changed. But note, in the meantime, that there's every reason for allowing investors to write off the cost of the loan. Take something like walnut – it's popular for furniture-making, and it takes

35 years for a tree to mature. And there are people who have borrowed to produce a walnut farm – that's 35 years of deductions before there's even a crop. The government's logic is elementary, and totally reasonable: no tax deductions, no walnut orchard, no jobs.

People in high tax brackets have always sought out this kind of thing, aware of the windows that investment can open. But increasingly these days, schoolteachers and other professionals, employed in fields where there are no tax deductions, are beginning to take a look. And with good reason: on average, we now pay 54 per cent of our income to one government or another. Every strategy has to take account of economic conditions. In times of recession, capital preservation is a better ploy than long-term investment. If things are looking dicey, you may say to yourself, ''I've built up this pool of money and I want to make sure I hold on to it until we get over the hump.'' Nothing says you have to be fully invested all the time. Nonetheless, even in tough times, the advantages of owning mutual funds or rental real estate are considerable. Property values tend to plug along even during bad times – if you're in a good location – and a mutual fund will too, if you've picked one that is not terribly risk-oriented. With real estate, whatever happens, you still have the assets, and, if you have to, you can sell. Likewise with a mutual fund, the fund will buy the stock. It's only a conduit. If necessary, it can always liquidate and you would get some of your money back.

Industrial Growth, for example, a very high-profile mutual fund, has done well in bad times through selling its stocks and going to cash. At the end of 1986, it was at 35-per-cent cash. In the late 70s, interest rates began moving upward, and normally when that happens, you expect stock markets to do poorly, so you preserve your capital. And yet, 1981 was Industrial Growth's only year of loss during the 70s and 80s. If you look at a graph of interest rates during the period in which they went up steadily, and then really took off, in almost every year Industrial Growth's return exceeded those levels. The numbers on the Templeton Growth mutual fund are even higher. Its worst year was also in 1981, when there was a 1-per-cent loss.

The interest on the loan to buy a piece of either one of those mutual funds would have been tax-deductible. And in all this, time is on your side. Even the people who had to survive through 1981, when interest rates were at their peak, saw that in 1980 they earned 29 per cent with TG. Mortgage rates were never above 20 per cent. So for one year there was a loss, but within the next two, the investors had more than got it back.

So in deciding how long to invest for, I always pick a decade. Nothing is cast in stone and if the world started to crumble, I'd probably sell, and take a loss if necessary so as to preserve my capital. But most people don't realize it only took about 2 1/2 years to recover from the crash of 1929. Look at a chart of the New York stock exchange and see what would have happened to $100 that was invested in 1871, then switched into United Mutual Funds in 1958, compounding all the while. With all the ups and downs that $100 today is worth more than $1,900,000. People blew their brains out in 1929, but 1929 was a blip, a short-term calamity. It's the big cycle that counts.

So a dip in yield should not be cause for alarm. When you SHOULD get worried is if you realize you've over-extended yourself. So be careful of overzealous salesmen, especially in real estate, and don't dream of going into something unless you know you can absorb any difficulties. Don't gamble, unless you can afford to lose.

The whole strength behind this is that it's a kind of forced savings plan, and if you don't have one you'll never get ahead except by winning the lottery. But don't do any of it without getting professional advice. It's too serious. It doesn't have to be that expensive – your lawyer and your accountant between them should know enough, and there's also been a tremendous growth in the number of independent financial planners. What we're talking about is borrowing money and going into something that you're comfortable with and that will normally take care of itself. The value of going in with a professional is that he's seen it all happen before.

In the case of a mutual fund, seek out the advice of an independent financial planner, somebody who sells everything, rather than an individual selling his own product, who will have an axe to grind.

As to whether you should consider lending money to someone who wants to make a mortgage tax-deductible, in general the answer is don't, except perhaps to a relative or close friend. You're not a bank, which has seen a million clients go through its doors and learned from their mistakes, and essentially you'd be doing things backwards. Interest-bearing investments are simply a mirror of inflation and if you lend somebody money, you're going to ask for a return slightly higher than inflation. The more interest you ask for, and are able to get, the riskier the loan is likely to be. Instead, buy the best investment you can. If the markets are in good shape, take advantage of that. If they're not, all the more reason not to take a chance on someone who wants to take a gamble with your money.

But there's two sides to everything: so, by the same token, if you do find a private lender willing to make the loan to you, you should consider taking him up on his offer because it may well have fewer strings attached to it than will a loan from an institution.

Chapter 3

Rental Real Estate: Write Off Everything

A lot of people are more comfortable investing in real estate than in stocks, mutual funds, or in a business, because they feel they can stay in touch more readily with the market. It's true, nothing is easier to monitor than house prices, especially in the immediate neighborhood. Yet owning and renting out a house or apartment is really no different than operating any other sort of business, except that it's perhaps simpler: you can automatically write off a portion of the interest on the mortgage, the taxes, insurance, heat, hydro, water – everything – as part of the cost of doing business. If you buy a house outright and rent it, then write off as much as you can: all the expenses associated with that project are tax-deductible. If, on the other hand, you own a basement apartment that occupies one-third of your own home, then one-third of the total expenses associated with running the house are deductible.

Automatically. You don't have to think about reorganizing the financing in the way we discussed in the last chapter. And money that is spent 100 per cent on the apartment is 100-per-cent deductible, aside from the case of the major expenditures, which we'll look at in a moment.

Perhaps you also use part of the house as an office, where you write books, or run a small lettering operation, or mail out circulars. Same thing – that's deductible, too. However, it's not deductible like it used to be, at least not for some people, because the home office was one of the targets Mr. Wilson took aim at in his reform package. Up until January 1988, the law still allowed you to deduct expenses arising from the operation of a home office, even where the office is incidental to the business rather than essential to it. Under the old rules, put simply, if you had a spare bedroom that you used from time to time as an office, but didn't actually require, that was okay. After that 1988 date, it isn't. Under the new system, you have to be able to show that you really need that space. A lawyer or an accountant, for example, whose principal office is outside his home, will no longer be able to claim any expenses for a home office unless he uses it solely for business and regularly meets clients there. A university professor, on the other hand, who runs a consulting practice out of her home, will have no trouble, and neither will the writer, providing they meet the other two criteria: 1) that the office is physically separate from the rest of the house, and 2) that there's actual income being generated. Whether it's a basement, a garage, or a fourth bedroom, the office MUST be a separate part of the house. The day of the kitchen-table executive is over.

But again, when we say an income has to be generated, that doesn't have to mean a winning income.

A person operates the rented apartment and the office on the same premise as with any other business: he probably does want to make a profit (not always, as we'll see), but if he's unfortunate enough to run up a loss, then he does everything he can to write it off. In fact, through a device called depreciation, which we'll discuss, it's possible to bring the tax payable on any income down to zero. This money might have to be repaid at a later date, mind you, if the building is subsequently sold (and we'll look at that, too), but in a given year, there's no reason why a rented apartment or house should ever have to operate at a net loss to the owner. And in the meantime, if it goes up in value 10 per cent a year, then it will double in value in 7 years. Meaning that when you sell, that's a tax-free capital gain, providing you haven't already used your $100,000 capital gains deduction.

For the person who already owes a substantial amount on his house, a rental property is probably the only way he can acquire a second one. Maybe, on the other hand, he just wants to add on to his house, perhaps by converting the basement or the attic into an apartment. Either way, the first consideration will be borrowing against the existing house. And perhaps there will be a net profit in the whole enterprise. If there is, then the wise investor will remember one of our basic tenets: use that cash to pay down the principal on the first mortgage. For a person already in debt, borrowing or refinancing to get further into debt might seem like going out on a limb. Talk to an accountant first, but in general, the well-run rental property represents an excellent investment, and for a number of reasons. Buying a duplex, no question, is the simplest situation. Half of it you live in, half of it is rented out. Right off, you'll be the owner of a bigger, and possibly much better piece of property than you could otherwise have afforded, while the net cost will be about the same. And it's not hard to understand why a person is further ahead owning a big $180,000 duplex, part of which he lives in, part of which is rented out, than in being the sole occupant of that neat, but rather small $100,000 bungalow down at the end of the street.

Look at the figures in the case of the duplex. Say you happened to have had a $40,000 down payment, plus the several thousand dollars needed to pay the land transfer tax (in those provinces where there is one), the legal fees, adjustments, house insurance, moving costs, and other odds and ends. You now need a $140,000 mortgage, so you shop around. Since the major lenders generally like the down payment to be at least 25 per cent of the selling price, and you don't have that much, then in this case the cost of the loan is a bit higher than you'd hoped, and you end up with a 3-year 11-per-cent $140,000 mortgage, amortized over 25 years. Excluding taxes and bills, that $140,000 loan calls for a monthly payment of $1,347. That seems high – until you take into account the rental income. The rented part of the duplex – maybe it's a self-contained, top-floor apartment – is only a one-bedroom unit, but it's spacious and the house is on a quiet, leafy street, 5 minutes from the bus, so say, for the sake of argument, it rents for $550, inclusive. That monthly income, which reduces the cost of the loan to about $800 per month, is effectively worth more than $55,000 worth of mortgage to you.

If, instead, you'd put down your $40,000 to buy the bungalow, you could probably have borrowed the balance at a more competitive 10 per cent. The $60,000 loan would still have cost about $536 per month. Taxes, of course, will be higher in the duplex, as will insurance, utilities, and everything else. But at the same time, there will be all kinds of tax writeoffs available, none of which are open to the owner of the bungalow, if he has conventional financing. In any sort of long-range scheme of things, you'll be further ahead with the duplex. And if you subsequently want to sell, and if the housing market happens to have taken a turn for the worse, perhaps because interest rates have moved up, then the income from the rental unit can look attractive to a prospective buyer.

This is the classic situation of a mortgage going to work for you, rather than the other way round. As long as that house increases in value, and in the long term most do, that tenant is doing you a big favor. He gets a place to live, you get an investment that appreciates. In a given market, all real estate rises in value by approximately the same amount. Say a year passes, everything's gone up by 10 per cent, and you decide to sell that $180,000 duplex. It'll put $18,000 in your pocket, instead of the $10,000 you'd have made on the bungalow. Deduct the extra $264 per month that the loan has been costing, plus the extra costs incurred because the building was bigger, perhaps an extra $3,500 in all, and balance that against the fact that you've been writing off half the operating cost of the building the whole year. All other things being equal, the duplex was easily the better investment.

Also, remember that the more you can spend on a house, within the middle area of the market, the better VALUE you're likely to get because there are fewer potential buyers. Pressure tends to be strongest at the bottom end of the market, especially when house prices are rising rapidly, as in the situation we saw in Toronto and Southern Ontario during the 1980s. There were an awful lot of people looking for $100,000 houses in Toronto. Unfortunately for them, such houses were few and far between, and, where they did exist, they usually came with a problem – such as location. In general, we can say that buyers at the lower end of the market, who can spend an extra $20,000 on a house, will almost always get more than an extra $20,000 of value. By paying more, you can almost always pick a better location, which in turn is not just more pleasant to live in, it's also a strong card if and when you decide to sell. An income property is thus a great tool for elevating a buyer above that bottom end of the market, for the good reason that although it may be a first-rate investment, there are always a sizable number of buyers who simply don't want the bother of dealing with tenants.

And sometimes, of course, they're right. Consider the question of bylaws for a moment. To me, renting out the basement of a house, or perhaps even just a room, represents a tremendous potential, but not always a desirable choice. Some local authorities don't always like you to have a tenant in your house – although try stopping it in a university town, especially near the campus. In a case like that, the municipality is compelled to turn a blind eye because it knows what horrendous sums of money would be involved in building extra residences. The same situation has prevailed in Toronto for many years, reflecting the city's acute shortage of rental accommodation: in 1987, there was a .01-per-cent vacancy rate, meaning that one apartment in 1,000 was empty (and the same applies in at least half a dozen other cities in Ontario) – giving the building inspectors little choice but to ignore the tens of thousands of "illegal" rental units.

For some people, in fact, the only way they can buy a house at all is by putting in that "summer kitchen," and they do so in the knowledge that bylaws are sometimes fuzzy. Fine. If you've got a boarder, or a couple of

students who don't race cars up and down the street at
2:00 a.m., then probably no one cares. At the same time,
however, a buyer who's looking for a rental property
would be wise to do so in an area that's zoned for it. You
can be sure that the lender will be interested in the legal
status of the property, and in addition to that common
sense tells you that in the long run a legal duplex or triplex
is bound to be a better investment than an illegal one.

Speaking of students, one result of tax reform is that
tuition has become slightly more attractive as a tax deduction. Previously, parents generally picked up the tab, and
it was not tax-deductible, but now students can claim their
tuition as a deduction. And if they don't need it, to reach
zero, they can transfer up to $600 in tax savings to a
parent's tax return. As well, the full-time student reduction
has been changed from a $50-per-month deduction to a
$10-per-month credit, also transferable. Now, that will
help matters, but it's still not going to pick up the whole
bill, and it gives fresh logic to an idea we've long
used, which is to buy a property for the child, in his or her
college town. The idea here is that the building is put in
the child's name, the parent rents it out to students, and
then installs his/her child as the manager of the building.
The rents now pay the manager's fees, and the manager
now has taxable income to pay for his/her own tuition.
But in fact that money is so little that it ends up producing
a tax deduction. And meanwhile, the parent will find there
are rental losses: and while tuition losses can't be claimed
as a deduction, rental losses can.

The real mistake that a lot of people make, however,
when they become landlords, is in deciding to cheat the
taxman by making the rent under-the-table income. This
is a bad idea, not just because those people are breaking
the law, but because they're often preventing themselves

from claiming all kinds of legitimate expenses – maybe even enough to create a net loss, which could offset other income. So there are two things to weigh here. As far as the bylaws go, look at what's happening in the neighborhood – and remember that bylaws, like anything else, can be amended; as far as the taxes go, do everything correctly and go by the book. Not least because if you fail to declare income and you get tripped up, which can always happen, you sow the seeds of trouble down the line – and you can find yourself having to defend and justify your tax return every year.

If, one way or another, you become a landlord, with income and costs, then that income, like any other, is subject to tax, balanced against your expenses. Remove the deductions and you arrive at the taxable net income. The big question that now arises is: how much can I write off? Go back to our duplex, but say that in this case, the building's not divided evenly in half. In computing just how much space the tenant occupies, you can do one of two things: you can compare the square footage of the rented property vis à vis the whole building, or else go by the number of rooms. And you can choose whichever is better for you. Revenue Canada's first choice is often the square footage, but that's not a rule that's carved in rock, and generally they will be amenable if you want to count up the rooms and do things that way. Let's assume you decide you can justifiably say that two-thirds of the operating costs of the building arise from the rental unit. There goes two-thirds of the interest on the loan, two-thirds of your taxes, heating costs, and all the rest. Plus there'll be the peripheral expenses, such as advertising for tenants, or the cost of chasing them out, which are 100-per-cent deductible. And in the case of insurance, you may actually be able to write off a bit more than two-thirds, as we'll see in a later chapter.

If, in the meantime, the expenses of running the apartment exceed the rental income, you may be in good shape. Why? Because that loss is now tax-deductible against your salary. The sad fact is that thousands of Canadians don't realize this and they don't use those writeoffs. They say: "Well, I didn't make a profit, I guess I lost." Not necessarily so. If you lose in a business venture, claim it! What do you think Dome Petroleum has being doing all these years? When you go through all the expenses and make out a tax return at the end of the year, you'll see that there's a place on the form for gross rental income and net rental income. So it may just be a simple case of saying you had $10,000 worth of income and $12,000 in expenses: okay, that's $2,000 you can knock off your taxable income that year. If you're in the 40-per-cent tax bracket, that puts $800 in your pocket. Now, some people will argue that you're better off delaying that $2,000 deduction until next year, when the rental income will be higher. I don't agree. I subscribe to the theory that you use every tax deduction you can. Why give the government money? You'll never get it back. And in the end, let's face it, you don't KNOW what's going to happen next year. If you have to, find a tax shelter next year, but claim the deduction now. Because who knows what bright ideas the taxman is going to dream up? And next year, don't forget, you can always borrow to buy another investment.

But what if you have more deductions than you can use? Say you're running at a major loss. It's a long cold winter, heat's pouring out of the windows, the tenants stiff you for a month's rent, insurance premiums take a hike, and then the pipes freeze. Bad news all round and it's costing a small fortune. A useful strategy in this case is to go and talk to the lender to try to arrange to pay extra principal against the nondeductible part of the loan, while leaving in place the tax-deductible part. Present it to him and he'll be open to the idea because what he gets out of it is a more secure loan. If two-thirds of the interest on the loan is tax-deductible and one-third isn't, it makes all kind of sense for him to let you pay off the nondeductible portion. One way of doing this is to set up a second mortgage, whereby the first mortgage is interest only and the second one is principal and interest. In fact, there are lots of instances in which a lender has done this. One of our cardinal rules has reappeared: use any spare cash to pay off the nondeductible part of the loan because there's infinitely more mileage in doing that than in paying down something that can, in any case, be written off.

On the other hand, what if you're making a net profit that you don't want? The example that springs to mind is that of a newly renovated apartment with a high rent and a big mortgage on the whole building. Because there's little or no maintenance, there are no deductions, and when it's tax time – at which point the rental income must be declared – then the whole enterprise is liable to end up costing a wad of cash. And, as we said at the outset, we don't have to let that happen. Enter depreciation.

A building – like anything else – "wears down." Anyone who goes house-hunting discovers that all those real estate clichés about "location, location, location," and "they don't make land any more" are true. The land DOES rise in value. The building, however, like any business asset, will deteriorate unless you stop it. Give it long enough and it'll crumble. Revenue Canada recognizes this, and the capital-cost-allowance provisions of the Income Tax Act permit a somewhat accelerated writeoff.

Under tax reform, there are now 37 categories of depreciable business assets, and the size of the capital-cost allowance in each group varies widely, from 100 per cent all the way down to the situation of a building which can now be depreciated to a maximum of 4 per cent a year – down from 5 per cent. And when money is being made on the building, depreciation remains a useful ploy. Take the same example of $10,000 and $12,000, but say that, instead of losing, you emerge from the year with a $2,000 profit. This year, then, you claim $2,000 worth of depreciation, and that money is tax-free. It's not really free money, it's more a form of saving, because the building really IS deteriorating: sooner or later, you'll need new shingles on the roof, and the wiring will have to be replaced. And I haven't yet heard of any home improvements that go down in cost. In the meantime, however, there's a writeoff that's extremely useful. Mr. Wilson cut back on it, but the basic principle underlying this particular tax break is unchanged.

If you use depreciation, it's important to remember that you can't go below zero: you can bring up your operating costs to the point where you don't pay tax on the rental income, but what you CANNOT do is manufacture a loss against your other income. So you go one route or the other, and depreciation is something to fall back on when the building is making money.

As long as the house is losing money, you want it to be doing so as a result of the ongoing expenses, because that way you can claim the loss. What you don't generally want is for it to lose money as a consequence of depreciation. This is because even though there'll be a tax deduction this year, and perhaps next year as well, all that money will eventually have to be paid back if and when the house is sold: the sum total of all the depreciation will be added up and balanced against the capital-gains exemption, in the same way that written-off interest costs are now under Mr. Wilson's new rules. For a person who is really strapped for cash, however (perhaps in the first year or two of a mortgage), that may be an acceptable long-term choice.

Another word of warning: some things have to be capitalized, rather than claimed as expenses. Lightbulbs, coats of paint, a new sink – those are part of the cost of doing business. Major structural improvements, however – such as the roof, a new furnace, or new wiring throughout – Revenue Canada regards as an integral part of the building, and it will require that an owner capitalize those costs, which is to say add them to the value of the building.

We've talked about sharing a duplex. But what about the person contemplating becoming an absentee landlord? There's no question that his best course is often to buy the house up the street, or a couple of streets over. Now, you may not want a rental property 50 yards away from your home, but it is the easiest to look after. The time and expense is less – you're cutting the grass, you cut the rental property's grass – and at the same time you can watch the house, knowing that the changing value of your investment will roughly parallel that of your home. It's also easier to keep an eye on.

But wherever the property is, and for whatever reason you bought it, it's either going to make money for you or lose money. Let's look more closely at the second situation, and apply some creative financing. In this case, say it's a $200,000 rental property that you want to buy. In your case, you don't have a lot of spare cash, but you do have $50,000 kicking around in investments, or in equity in your existing home. The normal way of doing things would be to cash in those investments, put the $50,000 down on the new house, and get a $150,000 mortgage. At 10 per cent, it'll cost $1,340 to service that loan, plus taxes and all the bills. So say you rent the house for $1,200 a month. With a bit of luck, and writing off as many of the expenses as you can, you manage to break even. Now that's all right, considering that the house is in all likelihood rising in value. But instead of going that route, why not use those investments – or that equity – as collateral to borrow the down payment?

See what happens now. Here you are with a $150,000 mortgage and a $50,000 loan, and say for the sake of argument that the best deal you could get for the loan was 12 per cent a year – costing $500 a month in interest charges, or $6,000 a year. In this situation, the building doesn't have a hope of making money. Not a prayer. If it was going to break even with $50,000 cash in it, then this time round it won't even come close. However, that $50,000 loan, which was taken out for the purpose of investing, is now producing a hefty tax deduction. Six thousand bucks' worth of writeoffs, in fact, which puts $2,400 in the pocket of a person in the 40-per-cent tax bracket, making the actual cost of the loan $3,600. If the house is then sold at the end of the year, with a profit of $20,000, then, with the rent coming in every month to cover most of the first mortgage, it will have cost that person a little over $300 a month to make 20 grand. Not bad for a losing proposition.

This sort of planning – constructive financing to ensure a financial loss – has always been a big thing with high-income earners, and, equally, it has always baffled some other people who fail to grasp how it's possible to make money through losing it. But you do have to make sure you're actually creating that loss, and that it isn't generated on its own. No one in his right mind is going to buy a property that by itself is going to lose money (unless zoning laws are going to change, or there is some other change afoot – which would make the buyer a speculator rather than an investor). If the property by itself is a loser, the buyer will be too, because he'll simply end up with tax deductions far in excess of what he can use. And he can also expect a suitably chilly response from any lender he approaches. A detail worth mentioning is that if you sell a rental property and buy another, some of the land transfer tax, legal costs, and real estate fees will be regarded as legitimate business expenses and tax-deductible.

In a moment, we'll look at what happens to the owner's tax status when the house is sold. But in the meantime, don't forget that if you install a tenant in your own house, your insurance is liable to be higher because you're renting to someone over whom the insurance company has no control. If you're not going to be living in the house at all, the cost of the loan may also be higher because the lender can take the position that there's a greater risk without anyone around to keep an eye out for such things as fire, flooding, and damage. In general, the bank much prefers an owner-occupied property. Plus, of course, there are all the familiar pitfalls of renting: the tenant who falls behind in his rent, then moves out without paying – or doesn't, which is liable to be worse. Then there's the aggravation of increasing the rent (be sure to take rent controls into account in all this, if they apply) and of knowing that you may have to drive across town at 3:00 a.m. with a toilet plunger.

But all that is overhead – part of the cost of doing

business. On balance, the benefits of properly managed rental real estate easily outweigh the disadvantages. In the end, you'll own that rental unit for one of three reasons: 1) you want to make a straight profit out of it, in which case you should make as large a down payment as possible; 2) you want to ride the market, and are content to break even in the meantime; as a rule of thumb, with a 25-per-cent down payment you can do that; or 3) you want to create a tax deduction to offset tax on other income. All three are viable ideas, all three work. It all comes down to the way in which a person uses the financing mechanisms that are available.

If you're contemplating a second home that is just that – a weekend cottage, for instance – then, wherever possible, pay cash, because a standard mortgage will not be tax-deductible, and almost any move that avoids the burden of the amortized loan is worthwhile. If you do have to borrow, it usually doesn't make any difference whether you use the cottage itself, or your principal residence, as collateral. The interest on the loan, and all the other associated costs, can only be written off if the second property is in fact a business, and is going to be rented out. However, as far as collateral goes, the nature of the cottage can make a difference to the lender: if it's in a remote spot, and appears for some reason undesirable, he may well prefer to use the principal residence as security for the loan, especially if the principal residence is rising in value more rapidly than the cottage. On that basis, he may also offer a better interest rate, and not require that the loan be insured.

Now, when we talk about the cottage being rented out, that doesn't necessarily mean 52 weeks of the year. Revenue Canada is not going to squawk too loudly if it's only occupied for 50 weeks; if it's rented out for only 5 weeks, on the other hand, then you can expect a pretty loud squawk. So, in general, you should consider renting it out if you're not using it – especially in the early years, when the bulk of the mortgage payments will be on the interest alone. However, it should be mentioned that if House A is your principal residence, on which there is an existing mortgage, and you borrow to buy House B, one thing you cannot do is then turn around, move into House B, rent out House A, and try to make the interest on the loan for House A tax-deductible. The crucial thing is the purpose for which the money was borrowed in the first place, and changing horses in midstream is not acceptable.

Whether the second house is basically for your own use, or whether it's a rental property, and if – like most people – you do have to borrow, it's often a good idea to borrow against your principal residence rather than against the property itself. Why? Because you'll likely get a better rate on the loan. If you do put up the second home as collateral, give some thought to borrowing locally: i.e., from a lender in the immediate neighborhood, who will have a better idea of what the land is worth, and who won't perceive the same risk that a banker who's hundreds of miles away might.

Or perhaps thousands of miles. For me, a second home in Florida – rented out when not in use – remains one of the best investments. And if it so happens that it's intended to eventually be a retirement home, in a great location such as Port Charlotte, then buying that piece of property today, at today's prices, makes it an even better one. You can get a loan in Canada – borrowing against your principal residence, or against other investments – to make the down payment and to furnish the property. And then you go looking for a second mortgage in Florida. This is necessary because, technically, a Canadian lender can't – directly – put out funds with a foreign property as collateral, which is a topic we'll look at more closely in the chapter on creative uses of RRSPs.

For the person who buys a second home in Florida, and obtains the mortgage there, something worth noting is that he has a certain measure of additional security. If things don't work out – if property values were to take a dive for example – the Florida bank would have the property to take back, but it would have an extremely tough time trying to sue, and if you doubt this, just try suing someone in the States. But that's a highly unlikely scenario. Florida is the fastest growing state in the Union, and come the year 2001, projections are that only California and New York will be richer. In the meantime, if that second property is a legitimate investment, with a reasonable expectation of making a profit, then the Canadian mortgage used for the down payment is worth all kinds of tax writeoffs, and so too is the FOREIGN mortgage; it simply doesn't matter where the money was borrowed. Yet many people fail to make use of this fact and are astounded to hear about it. In exactly the same way as with our duplex, we take all the income earned and balance it against the costs and, where necessary, we can use depreciation and all the other strategies that we've discussed.

Another reason to opt for the Florida condominium or bungalow, rather than the weekend cottage in Northern Ontario, or the B.C. Interior, is that it tends to be a much more viable business proposition, not least because it's a great deal easier to rent out. For anyone seriously interested in buying one, a company I have dealt with, and can recommend, is Port Charlotte Florida Homebuilders, in Burlington, Ontario.

Selling

So you move along, steadily writing off the business portion of the building, and then, for whatever reason, it's time to sell. Maybe that's what you'd been planning to do all along, or maybe you decide that Florida's too hot. Assume that property values have been moving up and you make a reasonable buck from the sale. Now the big question: how much income tax do you have to pay on that loot? Up until capital-gains tax was scrapped in the 1984 budget (taking effect in 1985), in most cases 50 per cent of the profit, after all expenses had been deducted, was added to a person's taxable income, and he would pay tax on it at his going rate.

This did not – and does not – apply to a person's principal residence, which has always been exempt from capital-gains tax, if it rose in value and was resold. But a secondary residence, or an income property, is something else. In that 1984 budget, introduced with great fanfare, exemptions were introduced whereby Canadians were to be allowed $500,000 in tax-free capital gains over the course of their lifetime. Now Ottawa has backtracked, and, instead, most people will see their exemption capped at the 1987 level of $100,000 and be hit by taxes on any gains beyond that amount. (The only exceptions are in the case of small-business shares, and the sale of farmland, for which the $500,000 limit still applies.) Under the new rules, not only is the total exemption itself lower than it was going to have been, but any losses that have been incurred and written off – such as interest costs – must, on the day of reckoning, be added up, and the exemption will be reduced by that much. In addition to that – in the event that the exemption has been used up, and tax has to be paid – the actual tax bill is now going to be higher. Instead of taxing 50% of the nonexempted gains, the 1987 white paper increased the rate to 66 2/3 in 1988 and to 75 per cent after the beginning of 1990. So that represents quite a change. Most home-owners are still unlikely to use up their tax-free capital-gains status, despite the new limits, but for the owner of an apartment building it's going to be a different story.

All the same, the new capital-gains rules are still going to produce a substantially lower tax burden than would be the case with sinking money into Canada Savings Bonds, or term deposits, or GICs. Because in those instances, 100 per cent of the yield is going to fall under the taxman's axe.

If the house – or PART of the house – is not your principal residence and you sell it, you have to declare the capital gain, even though you may not pay tax on it. What happens, in effect, for someone who's still within the $100,000 limit, is that he pays capital gains and then immediately gets it back; you put it down on page 1 of your tax return and remove it on page 2. And it might well be that a person doesn't want that to happen. Why? Because by being temporarily moved into a higher tax bracket, he can find that his child tax credit, sales tax credits, medical deductions, provincial tax credits, and a host of other things are all affected. He's better off not having the thing on his tax return at all. It was true before, and it's true now. One of the chief components of the Wilson tax package was a changeover from a system of exemptions to a partial system of credits. Whereas exemptions reduce the amount of income that is subject to tax, the new tax credits, which are worth the same to everyone regardless of income, are applied directly against the final tax bill. Deductions such as the personal, married, child, tuition, and charitable contribution became credits. So did the old-age and pension-income deductions, and it's been estimated that senior citizens on average saw their tax bill fall by $550. This change is the component that allowed the government to announce that 4 out of 5 Canadians paid less income tax than in the past. But it is just a partial change. In the case of the important tax credits, such as those in the first group that I listed, nothing has altered. And even though the number of income-tax brackets has been reduced to 3, from 10, under tax reform, the name of the game is still to keep the gross total income as low as possible.

Going back to our duplex, say for the sake of argument that $100,000 is the profit you make on this building that's been 70 per cent your principal residence, and 30 per cent a rental unit. Even though the apartment upstairs, or in the basement, has been a commercial proposition – it helped pay the mortgage, created tax writeoffs against your income, and enabled you to own the house while it rose in value — the whole profit is still BY ITSELF effectively tax-free, within the capital-gains limits, i.e., below $100,000. However, the $30,000 portion deriving from the rental portion of the unit will be regarded as earnings, and whether you've used up your exemption or not, you can be almost certain that the $30,000 capital gain will put you in a higher tax bracket, albeit only briefly.

So it can make a considerable difference whether or not a building that's sold is claimed as a principal residence (in a moment we'll look at one or two options). On the other hand, maybe you don't want to sell the duplex. Perhaps, instead, you've had another child and decided you want to take over that third-floor rental unit. If you do that, remember that that amounts to the same thing as selling it to yourself: you've bought it from a business for your personal use. And it now becomes taxable. Whatever appreciation there was in the name of the business is now subject to capital-gains tax. The same would apply where a family has a country cottage that they've been renting out, and to which they now decide to retire, making it a principal residence.

In the case of the weekend cottage, or the Florida condo, the fact that you don't spend a lot of time there doesn't disqualify it from being classed as a principal residence. Or let's say you rent an apartment downtown and also happen to own a ski chalet. You go there all winter, you don't rent it out much – and as we've seen, if you only rent it out occasionally, Revenue Canada sees this as just recouping part of an overall operating loss, and tends to turn a blind eye. In either case, when the time comes to sell, it's still possible to claim that second home as a principal residence – regardless of whether you actually live in it or not. Clearly, on the other hand, you can't do that if the place is rented out for most of the year and in the meantime generating useful income tax write-offs: in that situation, the taxman, unsurprisingly, regards it as a business, and, in the event that you sell, you'll either use up some of your capital-gains exemption, or actually pay tax.

Another question that arises is whether the tax-deductible loan hurts the status of the principal residence. The answer, in a word, is no. The fact that the house was lodged as collateral doesn't make any difference.

People also ask whether a house can be moved back and forth between husband and wife, without creating a tax burden. The answer is yes.

For the person whom we can term the "frequent seller," there are a couple of other things to remember here. If I buy a house, live in it, and then have to relocate, making some money in the resale, Revenue Canada is understanding enough; we're all entitled to do that once a year or so, no question. But when you're liable to run into a problem is if you do it all the time. If I buy House A, gut it, renovate it, push up the selling price, then move on to House B, do the same thing to it, then move on to House C, the taxman will take a good hard look at what I'm doing. Because in this case, I'm CREATING the increase in the value of the house, rather than simply benefiting from it. I'm not investing, I'm in business. The difference is crucial, and it's one that Revenue Canada is acutely aware of, because the increased value in those houses, once I've finished with them, is in fact my income – even though it may be a second income, because I do all the renovation work at night when I've come home from the office. And now that Ottawa isn't getting the capital-gains tax that it used to, it's all the more vigilant toward people who renovate houses and move on, constantly claiming, all the while, that this is their "principal residence."

And that's why, in the end, it's sometimes better for the person who's borrowing money and lodging her house as collateral to invest in stocks and mutual funds – to invest in a third party. Because somebody else – the portfolio manager – is going to make the fund rise (we hope), and thus the investment exists at arm's length. You as an individual have little bearing on what happens to it, other than having been one of the people who bought into it. And that means that as an investor, you're eligible for dividend credits that are not available to the person who's constantly sinking his capital into property, and reselling. That's not to say it's not worthwhile to invest in real estate on this basis. It is. And it may well be that there are justifiable reasons why a person has to move more than once in a year – and each time make money on reselling his house. But he should be aware that if he does, there's a good chance that he'll trigger an audit.

It used to be the case that where a family owned two pieces of property, one could be in the name of the husband and one in the name of the wife. That way each could be claimed as a principal residence, and capital-gains tax was avoided. Ottawa saw through that, and stopped it. These days, the fact is that in this situation, you're better off if you're not married to your spouse because sad as it may seem, this is one instance where non-married people fare better at the hands of the taxman. If Jack and Jill live common law, Jack can own the principal residence and Jill the family cottage. They can sell both and not pay a nickel of capital-gains tax; if they're married, they're only entitled to one tax-free principal residence.

And sometimes it happens that they have to sell both properties. Maybe they're relocating, for example, and have no choice but to get rid of the country cottage as well as the city apartment. What should they do? The answer is: get an appraisal on both, see what has happened to each in terms of appreciated value, and decide which of the two they want to claim as the tax-free principal residence. Because in the case of those who have used up their capital-gains exemption – which is going to be quite a few more than was the case before tax reform – the savings here can be substantial. So sizable, in fact, that some people in this situation have been known to split up, divide up the family wealth, sell it off – and then have an amazing reconciliation. But instead of dividing up the family, why not divide up the income?

Chapter 4

Income-Splitting

In the United States spouses have joint tax accounts and joint tax returns, whereas here we're taxed individually. The trouble is the standard deductions don't come even close to compensating for that. If a spouse earns more than about $5,000, he or she is lost as a tax credit. If a husband earns $50,000 a year and a wife $10,000, you can be sure they're going to put an awful lot more cash into Revenue Canada's pocket than if they each earned $30,000. An individual who earns $50,000 and who has a dependent pays on average about $5,000 more in taxes than the family next door with two working spouses, each of whom earns $25,000 a year. That's why it's become common for good tax planners to try to move money from the high earner to the lower earner, whereby the money is 1) initially taxed at a zero rate, until the lower earner crosses the no-tax line, and 2) is subsequently taxed at a lower rate than that to which the high earner would normally be subject.

There used to be a whole range of ways to capitalize on dividing the family income between a high-earning and a low-earning spouse, but this is one area where Ottawa has woken up a bit and plugged some of the loopholes. No longer, for example, can the high earner simply give money to the lower earner to invest, a strategy that – until the rules changed – meant that the family investment income was taxed at the lower earner's tax rate. It's still true, however, that if two spouses work, there can be a net gain by having the lower earner pay most of the family expenses. And with real estate, there are still a lot of useful devices that can be brought into play.

Say a husband and wife jointly own a property and they sell it for a net profit of $100,000; it doesn't matter what they paid for it. They decide they've had enough of being homeowners for a while, so they rent an apartment and EACH take their tax-free $50,000 and invest it. They'll BOTH now earn a dividend, which may not be taxable, plus they'll each get the standard personal tax credit – although no longer, as we've noted, does that include the first $1,000 worth of earned interest. It obviously makes sense to do things that way, and yet when it comes to selling a house and then renting accommodation, a move that a lot of senior citizens make when they retire, it's surprising how many couples stick to the old way of thinking that puts everything in the husband's name.

It's a very costly mistake. By dividing up the proceeds of the house and investing the money separately, the tax bill will be smaller because both people will be in lower tax brackets – as with our example of two spouses who each earn $25,000. Added to that is the fact that most pensioners can't claim their spouses as a tax credit because the spouse gets Canada Pension Plan, or old age security, and, as a result, has too much income.

That's straightforward enough. But what if they want to buy another house? In this case, an excellent move is for the husband to take his $50,000 and use it as the down payment, while the wife invests her $50,000. What we've done here is to legitimately move $50,000 into the wife's name. Revenue Canda can't argue with us because the basic property law says that she's entitled to half of the family house, regardless of whose name it's in. Income-splitting is still alive and well.

But what about the mortgage in the meantime? As we know, a mortgage is not normally tax-deductible, so effectively the mortgage bill is going to come out of the high earner's pocket. But where a family can save money is when a portion of the mortgage is paid down, and the money borrowed again to invest – as described in our first chapter. In this case, it makes lots of sense for the investments to be in the lower earner's name.

Then there's the situation in which a mortgage is locked up – no extra payments can be made against the principal. Here, the high earner should clearly make the monthly payment because by doing so the lower earner is free to invest. In general, what has to be done is to compare the real rate of return of a given investment with that of the mortgage. If a person has accumulated $10,000, which is earning 10 per cent, after tax, then that's a real 10 per cent in his/her pocket. If the family at the same time has a 9-percent mortgage, then it's clearly ahead. If, on the other hand, that investment income is taxable, then the whole thing may amount to a losing proposition – the investment is being robbed by the cost of the mortgage – and that person would be better off putting the money directly against the mortgage, and paying it down. In a nutshell, balance the after-tax rate of return from the investment against the out-of-pocket costs of the mortgage: if I earn $10,000 and I'm in the 30-per-cent tax bracket, then I'm really only putting $7,000 in my pocket. And taking everything together, it should be possible to invest at a higher rate than that of the mortgage. If you look at the track record of one of the good mutual funds – Industrial Growth, Templeton Growth, United Accumulative – then you're looking at a yield, on average, of at least 15 per cent. And these days, there aren't many mortgages that expensive.

Let's go back to the couple who have sold their house and are now looking at buying another. The wisdom of cashing in investments to make a down payment on a house or to pay down part of a mortgage is one of the premises on which this book is based. But perhaps a person doesn't want to part with his investments. Maybe they're too good. If that's the case, is there any reason why he shouldn't sell them to his spouse, paid for with her share of the house money? If that's what they do, then they keep the investments and they also have cash to buy or make a sizable down payment on the new property. Simple as this is – because all that's involved is transferring the investments from one name to another, without stockbroker fees – it's a move that's constantly overlooked. And once again, it's a completely legitimate way of shifting assets.

In the same way, what if a person doesn't want to sell his house at all? As we've said, the basic law of property decrees that each spouse owns half of it. So if your wife owns half the house, what if she decides to sell it to you, for cash? Say you happen to be in the position of having a tax burden: you've got Canada Savings Bonds, term deposits, whose yields are being taxed. What you could do in this situation is cash them in, give her the money, and thereby enable her to sign over her part of the house to you. And with that money your wife could, if she chose, buy investments. Good idea. And what better investments to buy than the ones that you have to sell? Maybe that sounds suspicious, but there's nothing startlingly original here. Business people move property back and forth between husband and wife all the time, perhaps because they need some collateral for something. The difference in this case is that it's being done for tax purposes.

Finally, there's what we can call "deep-freezing an estate in reverse." In this case, let's say that in addition to your principal residence you also own a cottage. You know the cottage is going to be part of your estate when you die and that it will be regarded as a capital gain if you sell it. And conceivably you've used up your capital-gains exemption. Well, what if it so happens that you have a maidenly aunt who really likes the cottage? To the tune of about one day a year. The aunt, by the way, doesn't own a principal residence – she rents an apartment. Why not sell the cottage to her? If she buys the cottage, then all future appreciation will be in her name – so that in the event that she sells it, there'll be no capital-gains tax. Auntie, of course, is old, so there's no way she can take care of the place. So she hires you to do so, and in exchange, you get full use of it.

On the other hand, maybe she doesn't sell it. Instead, because you've been such a kind nephew, she wills it to you – that's your share of her estate. Tax-free. Not everybody has such an aunt, of course, but as long as a person 1) doesn't have a principal residence and 2) hasn't used up his capital-gains exemption, he'll make do in a pinch. For that reason it's not an arrangement you would want to foist on a child because you'd be using up a highly valuable tax exemption, and later on in life he might not thank you for that.

Needless to say, everything we've talked about is strictly legal. The potential trap in all this, clearly – given Ottawa's stated goal of making the tax system more equitable – is that Revenue Canada will regard certain moves as being a sham. And that's why you might want to put some "breathing space" in these transactions – as discussed in making a mortgage tax-deductible in the first chapter. Precedent-setting court cases will undoubtedly make a difference, and so too, more than ever, will good records, good advice, and professional help.

Chapter 5

Compounding: The Growth is Spectacular

But let's pause for a moment. Why are we doing all this?
Why are we making such a point of counseling people
with equity in their home to make use of it through some
astute planning? The answer's not complicated. If you
look at, say, the Steel Company of Canada, which has
18,000 employees, then it goes without saying that the
owner of that firm – in this case the share-
holders – couldn't possibly do the work of those 18,000
people. And it follows that any time you can hire an
employee who does what he's paid to do, then even if you
only make 10 per cent on his labor, it's still 10 per cent you
wouldn't otherwise have had. And that's essentially the
way you should regard your money: as an employee. If
you do, then bear in mind that you face all the problems
that a businessman faces. But at the same time, you'd better recognize that in a sense you HAVE to operate along
these lines, especially when you start thinking about

retirement. Because the fact is, if you're content to just sit here with your nest egg of $10,000, or $100,000, quietly earning a modest yield in a savings account or a GIC, then it's impossible to make any headway. Indeed, a loss is guaranteed because inflation will combine with the tax bite, and these days we don't even have the $1,000 exemption we used to. And, as of January 1988, Revenue Canada is going to get a share of every penny of investment income. If inflation is running at 5 per cent, your $10,000 steadily falls in value by $500 every year, so just to stay where you are you have to earn $500 – before tax. Meaning that just to tread water you have to be able to guarantee yourself $500 AFTER the taxman has had his share.

That's assuming you're content to break even, and there's no doubt that lots of people only set their horizons that high because they say: "It takes money to make money and I don't have enough to be able to get ahead of the game." Well, that's often simply not true, and it's especially untrue if there are built-up assets that are not being put to work. The value in buying a house in the first place is that, as a principal residence, it rises in value tax-free, regardless of whether it's a million-dollar estate or a shack in the woods. And that's not just one house – it's as many houses as can be justifiably claimed. If you marry, then that's a justifiable reason for trading in the bungalow and moving into a 3-bedroom semi; if you get divorced, that's a pretty good reason for moving out. If you get transferred, same thing, and there's no reason why an individual whose circumstances match that scenario shouldn't own 3 different principal residences in a single year. The key factor here is that he's not manufacturing the increase in the value of the property: he's merely – because of circumstances – reflecting it. Whatever the time frame, it follows that the more constructively he can manage his mortgage, the more the appreciated value of the home will eventually end up in his pocket. In the meantime, the growing equity in the house can be regarded as an employee, who, if pointed in the right direction, can manufacture profits through investment.

So in the same way that the property produces tax-free compounding, what we should be looking for here is an investment that wherever possible does the same thing. Under tax reform, investment income is taxable from here to eternity – and if you think that's going to change, don't hold your breath. The lesson is clearly to steer away from interest-bearing investments, wherever possible. If you have a 9 per cent investment and you're in the 40-per-cent tax bracket, you're going to lose 3.2 per cent of that 8 per cent, providing a real return of 4.8 per cent. If inflation is also at 4.8 per cent, you've effectively earned nothing. To change that situation either the inflation or the tax has to be eliminated. You may say there's nothing you can do about inflation, but that's not really so because what you CAN do is seek out investments that historically outstrip the inflation rate. Real estate is the classic example, but mutual funds, antiques, and even gold will do the same. (Gold, however, has twin drawbacks: 1) there's not much you can actually DO with it, and 2) it produces no income.) Best of all is to buy something that does produce an income AND has the potential for capital appreciation, to offset the impact of inflation.

If, despite all this, you remain determined to go with interest-bearing investments, and so many Canadians will be because they love the word "guaranteed," then you should take notice of this tax change. We can compound for 7 to 10 years or even longer but we must pay tax each year as if we relieved the interest. In effect, interest income can be taxed in advance. You might die before you ever get your money but will have already paid the tax.

Going the interest-bearing-investment route is not the best we can do: we've got to be looking at something else. Even a piece of raw land. Far too many people are locked into the kind of thinking that demands that an investment produce a monthly, or yearly income, without stopping to think that if they buy something today that is going to double or quadruple in value down the road, then they've got their yield. History shows that if you buy something that's worth owning in the first place, it will almost always take care of itself. Yet Canadians are irrationally cautious when it comes to money, with more of it socked away in low-yield bank accounts on a per-capita basis than any other nation in the world. And I've seen and known literally thousands of people who receive interest income that they don't need. They buy a GIC, or a Canada Savings Bond, receive interest on it every year, and blithely plow it back in. And what I say to them is, "If you're not using it to live on, why don't you buy another investment? Because if you were to put that money into a piece of land, then unlike your interest-bearing investment, to which you're so attached, you'll never pay a dime in tax until you sell it."

So that's the first thing. And the second is that a non-interest-bearing investment is not taxable AT ALL until you exceed your $100,000 capital-gains exemption. Remember, however, that raw land is regarded differently from developed land in that the interest on a loan to buy raw land is not – in contrast to land with a building on it – tax-deductible. Which means that sinking cash into raw land may be well and good, but if you're planning to borrow, perhaps using your home as collateral, then that's a different story, and you should consider putting your money into something else. That something should 1) produce a regular yield, and 2) have some expectation of a future profit – a nice capital gain. That way, part of the cost of owning the investment, i.e., the price tag on the loan, is serviced. If you buy a Canadian stock or mutual fund, the interest on the loan to buy it is balanced against the income earned – and then the dividend tax credit kicks in, giving back some of the tax that's already been paid.

As we've noted, under Mr. Wilson's new rules, if you write off the cost of a loan every year, then that writeoff is carried forward and is eventually balanced against whatever remains of your capital-gains exemption. But that only applies to the amount of interest that's in excess of earned income. A natural situation would be to borrow, pay 10-per-cent interest, earn 10-per-cent income – and eventually get a tax-free capital gain; the interest on the loan and the income cancel each other out, leaving the capital gain with you. And under tax reform, this is going to become a common strategy; instead of borrowing and producing a tax deduction, while earning no yield, investors will increasingly make sure they earn enough of a yield to service the loan. And where the dividend tax credit applies, then despite its having been somewhat diluted overall, it's still pretty powerful. For some people, in fact, it's more beneficial than ever. In 1987, the person who's in the top tax bracket paid a maximum 23.1-per-cent tax on dividends; beginning in 1988, that same worst-case scenario was 19.6 per cent. So for that person, partly because tax rates have fallen, dividends actually became more attractive than before. After 1990, take any form of taxable income you can think of, and dividends are taxed at the lowest rate of all: lower than salaries, than interest – even lower than capital gains, once the exemption has been used up.

So the nub of all this is that if we can say to ourselves: "I don't need an investment that has a regular yield, instead I'll buy something that rises in value tax-free," then we're probably doing ourselves a big favor. But either way, the mistake people make is in thinking that this has to involve big sums of money. It doesn't. I was giving a seminar recently and a woman stood up and said: "I bring home 200 bucks a month more than I need to live on. What should I do? Right now, it all goes into the bank." She'd been doing this for 6 or 7 years, it turned out, getting regular raises at work and tucking it all away in a savings account. So we started doing a little arithmetic. That $200 a month is worth $2,400 a year to her and, at the end of the year, it's probably accumulated a total of $100 or so in interest. That's now instantly taxable, under Mr. Wilson's changes, but allowing for compounding then maybe at the end of 10 years her savings will be worth $25,000. But what would happen if, instead of waiting for 10 years to pass, she went to the bank and borrowed $20,000 on the strength of the equity in her home? If she did that, borrowing the money at 12 per cent, she'd have to pay $200 a month to service the loan. So come the end of the year, she'd have parted with the same $2,400 that she's depositing in her savings account – which, needless to say, the bank in turn is lending out again. However, a $2,400 interest expense on an investment loan produces a $2,400 tax deduction; in the 40-per-cent tax bracket, fairly average for Canadians, then the whole exercise is worth about $900 in tax rebates – cash. In this example, modest as it is, the woman currently makes $100 in investment income, which is then subject to tax. If she were to do what I suggest, she'd have $900 in her pocket. So you tell me which is better: she'd be 9 times ahead. But that doesn't even take the yield into account because meanwhile there's the $20,000 that's been put to work. If she were to take that 20 grand and earn 10 per cent with it, that's worth another $2,000. But maybe she puts her money into a good mutual fund and it brings a 20-per-cent yield: $4,000. There's tax to pay on that, of course, but so there is on all investment income. At the same 40-per-cent rate, she'll keep $2,400 of that $4,000. Add that to the $900 refund and you can see what's happening.

For a person with just $200 a month to spare, the investment probably should be a mutual fund, in fact, but it could be servicing a mortgage, too: the money could translate into a house that's $20,000 more expensive than the one you would otherwise buy. That lady had been stashing her money away for all that time – but what's the difference between saving it for 6 years or using it to service a loan for 6 years? The difference is that the second way is vastly more profitable, and that's why when we say that there's money in your mortgage, waiting to be made, we're very serious. Putting that $20,000 to work has a measure of uncertainty, as does any employee: some days he works well and puts in overtime, on others he's lazy. But the point is, he does work.

So what I'm really trying to stress is that this sort of financial planning does not have to be for the wealthy. The example we're using here involves enough equity in a home to act as collateral for a $20,000 loan, and that's a pretty modest amount of equity. Yet when it comes to procrastination, as a nation we could probably win the Olympics. It's an instinct that's very costly because the advantages of putting the pieces in place sooner rather than later are quite staggering. If I'm 30 years old and decide to salt away $3,000 a year every year until I'm 65, earning 9 per cent per year (please, try to earn more than 9 per cent), then that's going to turn into $705,373.83 by the time I'm finished. That's right. Thirty-five years worth of $3,000 contributions, $105,000 in all, will mushroom – in a tax-free environment – into more than $700,000. That's how strong the effect of compounding is and, if you want further proof, look at how amortization works because it's exactly the same process.

But what tax-free environment, you say? Good point, because if you're shelling out income tax on those gains each and every year, it's a very different story and, as we've noted, the tax on earned interest can only be deferred for 3 years at a time. And that's precisely the reason why you want to be earning that 9 per cent through appreciation in the value of land, or art, or inside an RRSP or Registered Education Savings Plan, where it will grow tax-free. Eventually, of course, the asset gets cashed in, and at that time, capital gains becomes payable, if a person has used up his exemption. But what has been achieved in the meantime is that the compounding has been allowed to take place unhindered.

As an illustration of the value of this, see what would have happened if that same individual had decided to make his move 5 years earlier, at age 25. That same $3,000 every year amounts to $15,000 worth of extra contributions over the 5-year difference. But the ADDITIONAL yield on the money, by age 65, is $399,501.20, putting the total at around $1.1 million – at a cost to him of an extra 15 grand. Now, if that fund of money represented the mortgage on a house – or, more likely, several houses, over the course of a lifetime – then that extra $3,000 a year, or around $250 a month, would have created an extra $400,000. If I subsequently sold the asset, and put the money into a modest 10-per-cent annuity, then that would give me $110,000 a year for the rest of my life, as against $70,000 a year, and all for the cost of $15,000.

Yet it's astounding how we fail to think in these terms, and the chief reason we don't is that we don't understand what's taking place – or could take place. But maybe you say: "I don't want to take on that $3,000 a year liability at age 25." Okay. Then try a $1,000 liability. Because you'll end up with more money doing that, at 25, than through pursuing the much more common strategy of investing $3,000 a year, but not starting until you're 40. Time is the crucial factor in hiring this employee and, because of the compounding effect, one employee at work for 40 years is going to be more profitable than having 3 at work for 25 years. It's that simple. That $1,000 a year – at our same miserly 9 per cent – will grow into a total of $369,000, for a cost of $40,000. And providing it's being used to service a non-interest-bearing investment, such as raw land, or part of a mortgage, then there'll be no tax paid on that money as you go along, and the interest can compound in the tax-free environment we mentioned at the outset. Prefer your RRSP? Then that will do the trick, too – and that's not taking into account the tax deduction that's attached to RRSP contributions. In the case of our $1,000 annual contributions: if you decide to wait 5 years until you're 30 years old, you'll save yourself $5,000 in contributions – and cost yourself $133,000 in lost accumulated interest.

What a waste – and it's especially a waste for the person who has equity in this home, but who in the early years had to sweat and scrimp to get the down payment, make the monthly mortgage payments, and to pay what extra he could against the principal. He does all that, finally starts seeing some light at the end of the tunnel – and then promptly sits back, instead of putting this great asset to work.

Take an individual who's say, 45 years old, reasonably

settled into his pattern of life, has a measure of job security, and does have access to a couple of hundred bucks a month he doesn't need. I'd like to have seen him start a lot earlier, but let's say for the sake of argument that he didn't. So he now decides to get things rolling and puts that $200 into a mutual fund, with an annual yield of 15 per cent. Most of the good-quality mutuals will average between 16 and 18 per cent a year – I would advise staying away from any whose track records show average growth of less than 15 per cent, or from any stockbroker who isn't getting you at least 15 per cent – but in this instance we'll be cautious and say that 15 per cent is all that he gets. Over the next 20 years, until he retires, his $200 monthly contribution is going to bring him a grand total of $282,744. Considering his late start, our friend could be worse off than having a quarter of a million dollars to supplement his pension.

And, as everyone with a mortgage should know, even a single percentage point will make a sizable difference to the figures, and so too does the number of years that we have this monetary employee on our staff. Going back to our 25-year-old, perhaps he can only manage to kick in $100 a month. That's not a great deal, and in fact over the course of the next 40 years, he'll make exactly the same total contribution – $48,000 – that the 45-year-old will part with over a 20-year period, putting away his $200 a month. If both funds are earning the same 15 per cent, then lo and behold, the 25-year-old will have accumulated – this is not a misprint – $2,455,143. Nearly 2 1/2 million dollars. Without spending a penny more, nor earning one iota more in the rate of yield. The difference is time: you've got to put your money on the line as early as possible.

And the reason you have to do that is that you KNOW

inflation is going to have an impact; all that's at issue is the question of how much. If you look at the chart on the next page, you can determine what your salary is going to have to be in future years – just for you to be able to stay where you are. Perhaps you believe inflation is going to run at 4 per cent. If you go down the left-hand column of figures, and find your current income, which is say $30,000, then you can trace the line across and see that 5 years from now you'll need a salary of $36,500. That's just to break even, ignoring taxes, new debts, or any other changes in circumstances. In 10 years, you'll need $44,407 – just to stay where you are; in 15 years, $54,000; in 20 years, $65,700. And so it goes – no less than the compounding of interest; it's remarkable how it adds up – and that's only a part of the picture because, of all the things that are guaranteed to happen when you retire, the most surefire bet is that your pension is going to be less than your salary. Maybe your pension will be two-thirds of the final 10 years of your salary – perhaps half of what you're making at the time.

However, that's with inflation just creeping along at 4 per cent. Go to 8 per cent – this too becomes a compounding process – and in 5 years from now, you can see that your $30,000 annual salary is going to have to be $44,080 if it's going to buy for you what you can get today. Now, maybe $44,080 is what you will be earning at that point, but if you're in any doubt you'd better start the ball rolling for yourself. In 10 years, you're going to need $64,768 in yearly income to stay put, and after 20 years the figure's up to $140,000. In 30 years, if our $30,000 salary is anything less than $301,880 we'll have fallen behind. Hard to believe but, unfortunately, true. And consider this. If you really are earning that $300,000 at that point in time, imagine how much you're going to lose

ESTIMATE YOUR INCOME IN FINAL YEAR OF EMPLOYMENT FROM THE FOLLOWING CHART

Current Income	Expected Inflation Rate	Years Until Final Year of Employment					
		5 Years	10 Years	15 Years	20 Years	25 Years	30 Years
$20,000	4%	24,333	29,605	36,019	43,822	53,317	64,868
	6%	26,765	35,817	47,931	64,143	82,837	114,870
	8%	29,387	43,178	63,443	93,219	136,970	201,253
$25,000	4%	30,416	37,006	45,024	54,778	66,646	81,085
	6%	33,456	44,771	59,914	80,178	107,297	143,587
	8%	36,733	53,973	79,304	116,524	171,212	251,566
$30,000	4%	36,500	44,407	54,028	65,734	79,975	97,302
	6%	40,147	53,725	71,897	96,214	128,756	172,305
	8%	44,080	64,768	95,165	139,829	205,454	301,880
$35,000	4%	42,583	51,809	63,033	76,689	93,304	113,519
	6%	46,838	62,680	83,880	112,250	150,215	201,022
	8%	51,426	75,562	111,026	163,134	239,699	352,193
$40,000	4%	48,666	59,210	72,038	87,645	106,633	129,736
	6%	53,529	71,634	95,862	128,285	171,675	229,740
	8%	58,773	86,357	126,887	186,438	273,939	402,506
$45,000	4%	54,749	66,611	81,042	98,601	119,962	145,953
	6%	60,220	80,588	107,845	144,321	193,134	258,457
	8%	66,120	97,152	142,748	209,743	308,181	452,820
$50,000	4%	60,833	74,012	90,047	109,556	133,292	162,170
	6%	66,911	89,542	119,828	160,357	214,594	287,175
	8%	73,466	107,946	158,608	233,048	342,424	503,133
$55,000	4%	66,916	81,413	99,052	120,512	146,621	178,387
	6%	73,602	98,497	131,811	176,392	236,053	315,892
	8%	80,813	118,741	174,469	256,353	376,666	553,446

through seeing your pay cheque suddenly replaced by a pension. You're going to be $150,000 out of pocket. Scary, eh? That's why you have to start planning – not next year, or the year after, but *now*.

And, for most people, a house is the pillar around which to organize that planning – both in the first years of mortgage management, and later on, when you can turn things round and hire some monetary employees. In the above case, we're looking at a 50-per-cent shortfall on annual earnings of $300,000. That's $150,000 you're going to have to come up with every year just to maintain your current level of purchasing power. Take whatever interest rate you choose; at 10 per cent, you're going to have to have $1.5 million invested to bring in that $150,000. And that's before tax. So this is not just sophisticated footwork we're talking about, this is survival – for a $30,000 individual, who's not exactly rolling in money by today's standards.

For someone who's better off than that, the figures start to become really dramatic. In 5 years, a $50,000 salary, at a low 6-per-cent inflation rate, will have to have grown to $67,000; in 10 years, $89,500, and on up the scale until we see that in 30 years it's going to have to be $287,175 to keep the individual where he is. Meaning that at age 65, when his paycheque is cut in half and replaced by a pension, he's going to need an awesome $1.4 million, invested at 10 per cent, to make up the difference. And that's before paying any income tax.

So take your salary, or its nearest equivalent, pick the inflation rate you think will apply and work your way across, remembering that if you underestimate inflation, the numbers are going to be worse than you project. And on that basis, you can begin to work out what your real financial needs are likely to be, bearing in mind all the time that a) these are all pre-tax figures, and b) come retirement, as sure as the sun comes up, your income is going to fall. There's going to be a gap, and the art will consist of filling that gap, but remember this is all based on the premise that you're happy to stay with the lifestyle you have now. If you're not – if you want to live better than you do now – then you'll have to plan better.

The trouble is, however, people rarely look ahead that far. Instead, they're content to sit for years on thousands, or tens of thousands of dollars worth of Canada Savings Bonds or GICs, which have no ability to increase in value to offset inflation. Those people get their monthly or yearly yield, faithfully put it back in the bank – and then they wonder why, in retirement, they have to struggle. They struggle because they're losing ground and because they didn't get started soon enough in devising a plan to turn things around. One definition of money is that the mint makes it first, but it's up to us to make it last. Old age is not the time to be discovering the truth of this.

Chapter 6

RRSPs and Mortgages

Registered retirement savings plans were among the winners under the Wilson tax-reform package. Even though there were delays in increasing the limit on RRSP contributions, the RRSP remains one of the most powerful tools at the disposal of the individual who has a mortgage. People often mistakenly think of it as simply a retirement savings plan, whereas – as financial planners know – it's actually much, much more than that. And in fact, tax reform has made it even more useful, now that interest on investments is fully taxable, and that there isn't the same scope for earning tax-free dividends that there was. In a nutshell what an RRSP allows you to do is to become your own banker.

To restate the general principle, an RRSP is a type of bank account in which a) interest is allowed to compound tax-free as long as the money stays inside the plan, and

b) for every dollar put in, the contributor is allowed to write a dollar off his taxable income, subject to ceilings that will increase each year until 1994. (The original plan called for the ceiling of $15,500 to be reached by 1991.) The RRSP is thus not just a rebate savings plan, it's also a vehicle for investment. I know people who have a couple of million dollars in their RRSP, but even where the amount is very modest, the same investment practices work.

For someone who doesn't have an RRSP but does have a mortgage, the question frequently arises: should I start an RRSP or put the money against my mortgage? I've done numerous computer calculations, using a range of different forms of assessment, and about 94 per cent of homeowners are better off putting money into an RRSP than paying down the mortgage. Since one of the premises of this book is that all mortgages should be paid down as fast as possible, that may seem like a surprising statement. But consider: if you're in the 35-per-cent tax bracket, then every dollar put in your RRSP (subject to the contributions limit) saves you 35 cents. If you put a dollar against your mortgage, you'll save whatever the interest rate is: if it's 10 per cent, that's what you'll save on the dollar. Granted, if you pay down the mortgage, you'll save money during every year of its life, but don't forget that as soon as you put the money in an RRSP it's compounding tax-free, and this will usually more than offset the gains of paying the same amount against the mortgage principal. So the way to decide is to balance your tax rate against the interest on your mortgage. Similarly, it's rarely advantageous to collapse an RRSP to pay down all or part of a mortgage because as soon as the money is removed, it becomes taxable.

Those who SHOULD pay down the mortgage are

therefore, firstly, earners in a very low tax bracket: for an individual in the 10-per-cent bracket, RRSP contributions are not going to save you a significant amount, if anything. Another situation is where one spouse is working full-time and the other part-time, earning too much for her (or him) to be claimed as an exemption – a point reached after the spouse has earned $500 a year, under the new rules. In this situation, a spouse earning $5,000 a year would do better to take some money out of her own RRSP (not a spousal RRSP) and pay down the mortgage because she doesn't need any of the RRSP-generated writeoffs. If she earns $500 or less in net income and has money in an RRSP, the money can therefore be used to pay down the mortgage without it affecting her husband's deductions; more than that and it will be taxed at the full rate.

The second group to benefit from using an RRSP to pay down a mortgage are those who are locked in at a very high rate. Even though that rate may be lower than an individual's tax bracket (with, say, a 17-per-cent mortgage and a 35-per-cent tax bracket), there will almost always be a net saving in knocking down the principal on a 17-per-cent mortgage because with monthly payments like that, almost the entire monthly payment is going on interest alone. Fortunately, the number of homeowners still stuck with that type of mortgage is now small.

In both cases, the yearly calculation is relatively simple, but where there is a high mortgage rate, use a loan progress chart (often included with a schedule of monthly mortgage payments) to see what will have happened to the principal amount of the loan, after a given period of time, by paying down the mortgage.

In general, however, put the money into the RRSP. This is therefore a key exception to our basic rule of paying off our non-tax-deductible loans, the rule having been overridden by the imperative of getting tax deductions wherever possible. And the best possible use for that tax deduction, when the cheque arrives, is to faithfully use it to pay off the principal on the mortgage. Say you're in the 35-per-cent tax bracket and you happen to have $1,000 lying around. You have a choice of putting the money against your 10-per-cent mortgage, and saving $100 this year, or putting it in your RRSP and saving $350. It's an easy decision – and it's even easier if you take the $350 rebate and put it directly against the mortgage. You've benefited twice: your mortgage is falling and your RRSP is growing.

But once the money's inside the RRSP, it's a different story. Borrowing from an RRSP to provide the funds for a mortgage, whether to oneself or to another party, can be one of the best moves to make because by doing so you effectively become your own lender. And like any bank, you want to build up a cash reserve as fast as possible: the more there is amassed, the more there is to draw on. If you decide to make your RRSP invest in a mutual fund that pays a 15- or 17-per-cent return, the accumulative value of that money, inside the RRSP, will provide an increasingly useful pool of cash from which to borrow. And yet there are thousands of Canadians who happily pay off their 12-per-cent mortgage, month after month, and then raid their 9-per-cent savings account at the end of the year (probably at the same institution) to make an extra payment against the principal.

If you decide to borrow from your RRSP to invest, for whatever purpose, it has to be from a self-directed RRSP – obtainable from a stockbroker, a major bank or trust company, or a financial planner. The fund has to be administered at "arm's length" by an institution – a trustee (and non-relative), and there are fees involved

($100 a year, generally, although competition is bringing the price down, and some brokers offer senior citizens self-directed RRSPs). A self-directed RRSP is the only one that allows the holder to decide where to invest. Because of the flexibility it allows, I can see the day where it will become very common.

The trustee must apply the same rules as any other lender, i.e., make sure the loan is viable and is secured by sufficient collateral. In the case of a mortgage, there is an additional administration fee, generally around $250, and you are also required to put CMHC or MICC insurance on the loan, the cost of which will be about 1 1/2 per cent of the mortgage value.

Adding up all these fees, and weighing them against generally low interest rates, a minimum of about $50,000 is needed inside the RRSP to make it worthwhile, so this is clearly not a ploy that everybody can use. When the rates were up at 18 per cent, the figure was closer to $30,000. The narrower the spread between the cost of borrowing from an institution and the yield on an investment within that institution, the more money is needed to make it worthwhile to borrow RRSP funds. With our $50,000 and, say, a 2-per-cent spread, that's $1,000 you can save yourself – less the fees. The spread tends to be bigger when rates are high, and the wider it is, the more attractive an RRSP-mortgage becomes. Now that any written-off interest costs have to be eventually accounted for, in the event of triggering a capital gain, under Mr. Wilson's new rules, the logic of borrowing from one's own RRSP is more compelling than ever. And as the percentage of capital gains that becomes exposed to tax increases, it will look still more so – meaning that that $50,000 benchmark will become less, even with stable interest rates.

Now, $50,000 sounds like a lot, but don't forget that

annual RRSP-contribution limits are going to be rising, although less rapidly than had been promised due to tax reform. The latest timetable calls for maximum RRSP contributions of $7,500 in 1987 and 1988, and gradual increases up to the 1995 ceiling of $15,500: $8,500 in 1989, $10,500 in 1990, $11,500 in 1991, $12,500 in 1992, $13,500 in 1993, and $14,500 in 1994. The overall limit on RRSP contributions remains at 18 per cent of earned income, while people who also belong to employer-sponsored pension plans normally are subject to additional contribution limits.

This new brake on contributions won't help any RRSP holders in their efforts to build a pile of working capital, but as a strategy, borrowing from an RRSP is as viable as ever. (The money can be accumulated faster, incidentally, if a husband and wife both contribute to a spousal RRSP; there's also the situation of the spouse who dies and passes an RRSP along; and as well, it's becoming increasingly common for people to transfer their pension funds into their RRSPs.) Clearly, however, if you're already earning 9 1/2 per cent on a term deposit and have a short-term mortgage at 8 1/2 percent, there's no advantage whatever in borrowing from yourself – not only would there be a loss, but there would be fees on top of that. Investing in a third party is another matter, which we'll look at shortly, but in this first situation you'd be far better off taking that money and investing it in something else. The spread is thus all-important in making the decision.

But where it is viable, the business of lending money to yourself has enormous advantages. If you go to a conventional lender, the first thing you'll be offered is a scale of rates – for 1-, 2-, 5-year terms, etc. But in the case of using a self-directed RRSP and becoming the lender, you can decide the terms. At the time of writing, in 1987,

6-month bargain-rate mortgages were available from most banks, but let's say something changes and no one wants to offer you a 6-month mortgage; if you're borrowing from yourself, you can get one. You can also give yourself an open mortgage – without any 3-month penalty clause – which is particularly useful if interest rates start falling because you can ride them down all the way, knowing that the day it looks like they've hit bottom, you can then either lock yourself into that low rate or walk into a bank and do the same with a conventional loan.

Or you could do things exactly the other way round. Normally, since the mortgage is not tax-deductible, you will generally charge yourself the lowest interest rate you can – you become your own preferred customer. What if, though, you're in a situation in which you are not able to put much money in your RRSP? You're already near the ceiling on contributions and you get a pension rollover, or some other lump sum. In this case, a strategy is to borrow from your RRSP at the HIGHEST rate allowable and immediately "top up" the RRSP, replenishing the borrowed funds with the lump sum. That way, the interest builds up tax-free, as long as it stays inside. If, instead, you were to simply put the lump sum in a savings account, you're going to be paying tax on the income it produces. And now, under the Wilson package, the first $1,000 of that income is no longer tax-free.

Or perhaps you might want to pay yourself interest only on the loan, rather than principal and interest. It doesn't matter. The point is, by having control over your RRSP, it becomes a tool. The only obligations are that you must make your payments on time and you must charge yourself the going rate being charged by an institution. If the bank offers, for example, a 6-month mortgage at 11 per cent and a 10-year mortgage at 13 per cent, you will have to charge yourself somewhere between those two. If you try to give yourself a 1-per-cent mortgage out of your RRSP, you'll be in for a surprise; similarly, you can't charge yourself 25 per cent.

But what if you borrow the money from your RRSP, and make the loan tax-deductible, in order to buy, say, some mutual funds? You do this by putting a mortgage on your house – or some other piece of property – and using the proceeds to buy investments. Whatever it is you invest in, as long as it conforms to the rules we discussed in the chapter on making a mortgage tax-deductible, then you can write off the interest on the loan. And clearly, in this situation, you'll want to pay the money back to the RRSP at the highest rate possible. The gains here can become really substantial because the higher the rate, the more you can write off, and the more will be accumulating within the RRSP – tax-free. Meanwhile, the investment itself is rising in value – also tax-free.

Borrowing from your RRSP for a second mortgage is a perfect example of the flexibility in intelligent financial planning. Say you arrange conventional financing for the first mortgage, paying the lender – as with any other loan – the lowest rate you can find. You still need funds for the balance, so you now tap into your RRSP nest egg. If it's to your advantage to lend yourself that cash at a high rate – perhaps because, even though the loan may not be tax-deductible, the compounding taking place within the RRSP still makes it worthwhile – then you can borrow at a rate 3 or 4 percentage points above that of the first mortgage. On the other hand, maybe you want to go the other route, and you want a low-interest second mortgage. You can do that, too – lots of second mortgages are at first-mortgage rates because the whole thing is based on the borrower's merit.

In considering borrowing from your RRSP to buy rental real estate, a key question to ask is: where is the property? Does it qualify for NHA insurance or insurance from the Mortgage Insurance Corporation of Canada, which you have to have. If you're borrowing to buy a cottage, it's conceivable you won't qualify, perhaps because the cottage is difficult to get at, making it a fire risk, or prone to flooding, or is in poor condition. However, if it doesn't qualify for insurance – or sometimes even if it does – there's nothing stopping you from borrowing against your home in the city to buy a cottage, rental property, or any other type of investment. In the case of a rental unit, in fact, it may well be advantageous to borrow against your own home rather than the rented one because loans against owner-occupied homes tend to be cheaper, as is the cost of any insurance on the loan.

Wherever the money comes from, there will be administration fees, NHA insurance, and legal fees, but don't forget that in the case of an investment, these all become tax-deductible. And so in this case, the $50,000 that we have said is the rough minimum needed, in 1987, falls to around $30,000.

Money accumulates inside an RRSP tax-free – but only so long as it stays inside the plan. However, by borrowing from that RRSP to make a legitimate investment – whether in property, stocks, or a business venture – what we've actually done is gotten out from under one of the burdens of the RRSP. We've managed to move the money out of the plan, allowed it to grow – and paid no tax.

In the case of investing in a business, there is still more leeway available if the business owns property. If it does, one option is for the business to borrow from the RRSP, using the business's property – perhaps the building in which it is located – as security. That way, you can lend out the RRSP funds without having to use your own home as collateral. The variables discussed above – fees, insurance, the rate spread – still have to be taken into account, but what you may escape is having to sign your soul away, which in the case of a small business is what the bank frequently wants. If the RRSP is lending to the business, and it gets NHA insurance, the business won't take the house with it, in the event of it going under.

What about borrowing from your RRSP to finance buying a house abroad? On the face of it, it can't be done, because only 12 per cent of the book value of an RRSP can be invested abroad. But look again. If it just so happens that your principal residence is mostly or completely paid for, you can use it as security to lend that RRSP money to yourself. And once you've done that, you can do whatever you want with that cash. As long as the payments are made to the RRSP each month, it doesn't matter where the money goes. The property could be a ski chalet in Europe, or it might not be real estate at all: it could be foreign stocks or mutual funds. What you cannot try to do, however, is borrow from an RRSP and put a mortgage on a foreign property – and this is an area where the law has real teeth in it: there are sizable penalties attached to making an illegal investment with an RRSP and it's a dumb idea to attempt it.

We know that an RRSP is far more than a fund of cash saved up for one's old age, so what better use could there be for it than to help finance a retirement home? As we noted in the last chapter, if you wait until retirement to buy the house, you'll pay that year's prices; property values go up and down in the short-term, but in the longer term they go in only one direction. Far better to buy the house now, rent it out, and let the tenants and the taxman pay for it – because, as with any business, there will be tax deductions. Right off, the fees will be deductible, as will the interest paid back to the RRSP, plus the cost of insuring it.

It's sometimes a mistake to pay cash for property – assuming one is able to do so – but in the case of a retirement home that you're NOT going to rent out, buying it outright is often a good idea because the mortgage is not tax-deductible. Most of us, however, do have to borrow, and in this case placing a mortgage on your principal home, switching that money into a self-directed RRSP, and then using it to finance the house in Florida is a great way to do it. On the face of it, it looks like a dodge, but it isn't because, although you've actually invested abroad, the security for the venture remains at home – in your house. All you're effectively doing is pulling the equity out of your home and using it – but without the banker. The RRSP, in fact, becomes the banker – and, as with any other lender, if you don't make the payments, the RRSP will foreclose on you. The difference is that instead of making payments to the bank, you're making them to yourself, where they steadily accumulate – tax-free. Which is the premise of this book: there's money in your mortgage.

I bought a Florida house in Port Charlotte, a single-family house, on the expectation that that was a better investment than a multi-family unit; plus I eventually plan to retire there. Rented out from time to time at $650 a week, it more than carries the mortgage payments and upkeep, and so the rest of the money is used to pay down the mortgage. My RRSP provided me with that house, and the interest on the money it so generously lent me is tax-deductible against my other income. And when the time to retire does arrive, a pleasant home in Florida – paid for – is going to be a lot more comfortable than a safety deposit box in cold, wintery Canada.

If you're considering buying a house like this, a word about timing: try to synchronize things with the date your mortgage is coming due. First, you may not want to have to break an existing mortgage to refinance; second, this is the time when the various fees are being paid anyway, so the additional cost may be small or nonexistent.

Remember, the Florida retirement house doesn't have to pay for itself in the years that you're still living in Canada. In fact, you may not even want it to. Say it's a $100,000 house with a $50,000 10-per-cent mortgage on it. Obviously you want to live in it for some of the year, so it's only rented out part of the time. The net result, when you've added up interest costs, upkeep, legal fees, ads for tenants, improvements to the property, etc. is a 50-per-cent loss: $12,000 a year in servicing the house, and $6,000 a year in rental income. That loss is directly applicable to the rest of your income: $6,000 that you would otherwise have paid tax on is now tax-free.

But what if you don't need that tax deduction because you've organized your finances properly and you've already got more write-offs than you can use? Well, if you've really run out of ideas, how about just taking the 6 grand back out of your RRSP and simply spending it? Normally you'd pay tax on that withdrawal, but in this case there's now a $6,000 deduction waiting to offset it. Again, what you've done is used the rental property as a door to removing money from your RRSP.

In the right circumstances, using an RRSP as a means of offering a vendor-take-back mortgage can be a good move, and it's one that's commonly used by real estate agents. Say you're selling a house for $100,000, buying another for the same amount, and the buyer of your house for one reason or another wants you to take back a mortgage of $50,000. For you, doing things out of your own pocket can represent financial suicide. First, you want to get rid of the house, and instead you're being tied to it. Second, and much more important, you're now probably going to have to borrow to buy the second house because you didn't get all of your money out of the first one. The interest rate for both mortgages could be identical – but the difference is the money on the income from the mortgage on the old house is simply regarded as income and hence is taxable. If those two $50,000 mortgages are at 10 per cent, the deal is going to cost someone in the 40-per-cent tax bracket $2,000 a year. And chances are the two rates are not identical – the one on the take-back mortgage will likely be lower. That's why you offered it.

But things can look quite different if you get your self-directed RRSP to offer the vendor-take-back mortgage because what you're doing in this case is making a legitimate investment. In this case, the purchaser writes a monthly cheque to the institution administering the RRSP and it goes into the account – tax-free. If you're not able to charge the purchaser the administration costs of the RRSP, as part of the mortgage, then make sure you write it off later as a deduction – paid for out of your pocket, not the RRSP, which doesn't need any deductions. The legal fees should be picked up outright by the purchaser – that's part of his cost of doing business, not yours. Also, there may be an additional saving in that you don't necessarily need NHA insurance in this case because you're taking your own chances. However, if you do insist that the purchaser take out insurance, and pay for it, so much the better because now you're protected against default.

If you're offering a vendor-take-back mortgage through an RRSP, you're often better off holding the second mortgage rather than the first one because the net risk is smaller. Also, you should generally offer it on a short-term basis, such as a year. That way you can get it over with: it may well be that you only took back the second mortgage because you had to, and you charged the purchaser whatever rate you could. A year down the road, when his financial situation improves, he'll have every reason to refinance elsewhere and you can wave goodbye to the second mortgage.

You still have to be careful, however, because if the purchaser of your house is going to default on somebody's payments, there's a good chance they'll be yours – the bank is likely to be more adept than you at making sure it gets its money each month. Banks tend to be extremely good at that. If the payments are not made on time to your RRSP, it will go into default, which will mean you'll have to sue. If there's been a large down payment, you shouldn't have too many worries because not many people are prepared to walk away from a house when they've got a lot of equity in it; as well, it's worth noting that the situation tends to be more viable if the purchaser and you are in the same locality, rather than at opposite ends of the country.

So you decide the risks are minimal and you remove the money from your RRSP to pay for the mortgage, charging the purchaser the going rate. Again, as with borrowing from an RRSP for one's own mortgage, this has to be done within the broad parameters offered by the lending institutions. But there is more leeway to charge a higher rate in this case because there is a third party involved – the "arm's length" rule. Similarly, in a time of high interest rates, when the banks' "spread" is wider, the lender has more discretion to offer a relatively low one – and that could be a deciding factor in the sale. During the horror days of 1981-82, when rates were at their peak, there were numerous real estate transactions that only took place because the vendor offered to provide some of the financing.

On the other hand, there might be little point in depriving the RRSP of money that could be producing a substantially higher yield – in a mutual fund, for example. As much as anything, it will depend on how badly you need to sell the house. For real estate agents, regardless of the state of the market, that need is usually pretty bad – no sale, no commission. Dipping into an RRSP is the thing that can often close the deal, especially in a red-hot market like that of Toronto this past year or two, in which purchasers' finances were frequently stretched to the limit. Many times, I've shown agents how to bridge a shortfall of a few thousand dollars by means of a third, 1-year mortgage out of their own RRSP. At the end of that year, the owner's equity in the house has probably increased and real-estate prices will likely have edged up. So for the agent the very worst that can happen is a forced sale – and another commission. Lots of agents lend buyers small amounts of "bridge" money on a short-term basis, but, equally, many make the mistake of doing it out of their pockets, rather than drawing from the RRSP. And it's usually a great investment. On a $100,000 transaction, an agent will generally pocket about $1,500 – a 6-per-cent commission split equally between the buyer's and the seller's agent, and then divided again between the agent and the company for which he works. If the buyer is short $5,000, and the agent lends it to him, it gives the agent a 30-per-cent yield. Plus she can write off the interest and any fees that the client is not paying. It's for that reason that I know of agents who have 15 or 20 mortgages inside their RRSPs, continually coming due, so there's always cash in the till to do another deal. And meanwhile, of course, that means that money outside the RRSP has been freed up for use elsewhere.

Another reason to make the loan through the RRSP rather than out of your pocket is that the plan, and its trustee, legally MUST receive its payments every month – meaning there's not much to talk about with the borrower should he start skipping payments because the matter is now out of your hands. To put it plainly, he gets sued.

A variation on the RRSP-based loan is when home-owners A and B each own a house in a subdivision. Both properties are dependable investments, both parties trust each other, so they invest in each other with money from their RRSPs, making the fees tax-deductible. And when the payment is made each month, it's used to buy into a high-yield investment, such as a mutual fund. This is clearly a far better deal than simply lending yourself the money, and Revenue Canada, needless to say, knows that too, and is liable to look at the whole thing as a scam: you're not investing, you're benefiting directly. As a result, one tactic that has become popular is for clubs to form, moving RRSP money along the line and round in a circle: homeowner A lends to B, who lends to C, who lends to D, who invests in A. The distance this puts between A and D makes this acceptable, and proof of a "direct benefit" becomes more elusive still if party A is lending to party H, who is eventually lent money from the RRSP of party W, etc. Meanwhile, everybody can dispense with the cost of NHA or MCIC insurance. It looks like a dodge, but con-sider: when you hold an RRSP with an institution and then decide to hit them for a loan, there's an intertwining there, too. So this "daisy chain" arrangement is acceptable; a one-on-one situation is less so and I advise against it.

Finally, we should note that in the case of certain, high-income earners, the rules are going to change. In addition to the other changes we've listed, members of defined-benefit company pension plans will have their annual contribution limits to RRSPs adjusted to reflect the plans' benefits. In the case of plans that provide low or moderate pension plans, and for individuals who do not belong to company-sponsored plans, the ceilings will increase: anyone earning about $50,000 a year or less, and who belongs to a plan with moderate benefits, will be further ahead. However, the pension-adjustment formula that has been proposed, based on a sliding scale of earnings, will paint a different picture for the high-paid executive. By 1995, the individual earning $100,000 a year will, like everyone else, have an RRSP contribution limit of $15,500. But at the same time, a new adjustment formula will reduce that. That's a change designed to make the RRSP rules more equitable. For people with good company plans, it will somewhat complicate things.

So there have been changes about how much money can be put into an RRSP, and when. The net result, for most people, has been negative. But that's only compared to the way it was. The RRSP remains one of the best investment devices available to Canadians. Yet all too often it just sits there, quietly growing, and doing nothing else except getting older, as if it were in retirement itself. If you go to work, why shouldn't it?

Chapter 7

Vendor-Take-Back Mortgages, "Granny" Mortgages, and Investing in Mortgages

Vendor-Take-Back Mortgages

The 1981-82 period of sky-high interest rates was the most recent heyday of the vendor-take-back mortgage. During the surge in house prices in Toronto and Southern Ontario in the past couple of years, where the momentum was largely generated by the steady fall in the bank rate, they became relatively rare, simply because the bank was often the cheapest place to go for a loan. Any significant upward shift in the bank rate, however, and VTB mortgages will likely become more popular than ever, at least within a hot market area, for the good reason that when prices are high, a 1-per-cent difference in the cost of a loan can become crucial to some buyers.

101

In general, we know that a VTB mortgage usually works to the purchaser's advantage, and hence is used by the seller as an inducement to buy; so let's first look at it from the purchaser's point of view. The advantages of a lower interest rate speak for themselves, but there may be more here than meets the eye. What if the buyer was able to make that VTB mortgage tax-deductible? Revenue Canada will normally tend to look at a VTB mortgage as a straight loan, with no deductions allowed for any of the interest paid every month. But there's a way around this: the buyer (borrower) liquidates whatever assets are at hand to buy the house outright, or to make as big a down payment as possible. And THEN he borrows money from the vendor, on the best terms possible, as always. And he re-invests, in stocks, a business, or some other legitimate enterprise that will qualify the loan to make it tax-deductible. Once again, we must mention that because of uncertainties that have been raised in the wake of the Bronfman case, the safest way of doing this will be to put a little distance between the transactions. But as a tactic, it's still alive and kicking.

Needless to say, most people aren't in a position to pay cash for a house – that's why they're borrowing the money in the first place. But the point here is that you still make just part of your mortgage tax-deductible – and it should be as big a part as possible. All too often, a person who is buying a house and who has investments elsewhere decides, for the sake of "security," to treat the investments and the mortgage as different creatures. They're not. They're all components of that person's financial situation and, by cashing in the investments and then borrowing to buy investments back, they've actually become more secure than they were before because the person's overall situation has improved.

For the vendor in this situation, a VTB set up like this becomes just a technicality, a matter of rewording, because all the purchaser is essentially doing here is putting up cash in lieu of that second mortgage. And, as we know, he's probably getting the vendor's loan on much better terms than those being offered at the bank. In 1981, when interest rates were in the 18-per-cent plus range, there were any number of 12-per-cent VTB mortgages around. So potentially advantageous was this situation, in fact, that there were instances where people were selling their houses to buy another one – just to get that low-cost loan. And you can be sure that Revenue Canada was frequently sending in its team of parachutists because crisscrossing loans with investments has all the appearance of being a tax dodge. But whatever Mr. Wilson may think, tax-saving devices are in fact part of what taxes are all about. The courts have always upheld this notion, yet some people persist in thinking that perhaps everyone is not supposed to know about ways of minimizing the tax bite. And maybe there's a grain of truth in that – which is perhaps the reason that financial planning is a growth industry.

Here's a classic situation. I once bought a house at the same time that I was buying an investment – an Income Averaging Annuity Contract, which is a tax-saving device that was useful when you had a windfall, or an irregular earning pattern (as is the case with writers or athletes) and wished to spread the tax bite over future years. In my case, both the house and the IAAC had to be paid for at about the same time, so I paid cash for the house and had the vendor lend me the money to buy the IAAC. The annual yield on the IAAC was 18 per cent, and I bought it with money that I'd borrowed at 10 per cent. Meanwhile, I'd bought a house in a down market (it eventually doubled in price, a tax-free capital gain) and the interest on the VTB loan became tax-deductible against my other income. Now if you're paying off, say, a $60,000, 10-per-cent loan, that's 6 grand a year you can write off. For a person in the 40-per-cent tax bracket, that's $2,400 a year in savings – cash. Ottawa is now paying $200 a month toward that person's mortgage, which over a 5-year period turns into $12,000 worth of government money. A person in the 50-per-cent tax bracket would have to earn $24,000 to pocket the equivalent of that, so the savings here can become huge. There are thousands and thousands of cases where this simple, knowledgeable little transaction has been used – and an awful lot more where it should have been.

In my own situation, Revenue Canada came chasing after me, and they'd have been stupid not to have done so because it was a triple transaction, instead of the usual double transaction. They subpoenaed the bank records, the legal records, everything, and it all came out squeaky clean. So be sure to dot the I's and cross the T's because it becomes like a paper trail in which everything must go in the right order.

In the last chapter, we talked about RRSPs and the mechanics of using one to offer a vendor-take-back mortgage. But what if you have to offer a vendor-take-back mortgage – your back is against the wall and it's the only thing that will clinch the sale – and you don't have an RRSP? As we've seen, for the person who is selling a house so as to buy another, the standard VTB mortgage can represent a big mistake – double jeopardy – because he has to pay tax on that monthly income, while at the same time making non-deductible loan payments to the bank. But here's something I've seen done in the past and, as a strategy, it's one of the best.

Let's use the example again of a seller who's in the 40-per-cent tax bracket, who has his eye on a new property, and who needs to take back a second mortgage of $50,000 in order to unload the old property. Instead of you, the seller, lending the buyer the money and then borrowing it back from the bank to finance the new house (double jeopardy), you reverse the sequence of things: you borrow the money from the bank or trust company – and make that money available to the purchaser of your old house. He borrows the money, buys the house for cash, and you in turn use that cash to buy the new house, which becomes the bank's security for its loan to you. The old house changes hands, and every month the new owner sends you a cheque because he owes you $50,000. That of course is still income, but the difference is the interest on the money you borrowed from the bank has become tax-deductible. Effectively, what you have done is invest in the owner of your old house. And not a penny of extra money has changed hands – in fact, you'll probably come out ahead because as well as saving yourself $2,000 a year in the interest on the loan (for a person in the 40-per-cent tax bracket), you'll also have charged the purchaser the legal fees.

Now, this is the way I've seen things done in the past, but because of the doubts created by the Bronfman case, this might be an instance where you may want to be sure to "insulate" the transaction. The question also naturally arises: since the purchaser is probably going to want you to give him a cheaper loan than he could otherwise get, what if you have to borrow from the bank at, say, 12 per cent, and then lend it out again at 10? Will the bank accept that? The answer, most likely, is yes because as long as you're able to make your payments, and as long as collateral exists in the form of your new house, there's no reason to refuse. In fact, you're a better customer because you now have $2,000 you would otherwise have forked out to Revenue Canada.

People who sell off their house in order to live off the money, such as individuals who are about to retire, often find it expedient to offer a VTB mortgage to the purchaser. There's nothing wrong with that idea, providing they've received a good down payment and have confidence in both the buyer and the house itself – i.e., that despite having risen in cost the property is still a good investment for its new owner. The mortgage payments now supplement their pension. The drawback here, however, is often that the seller then moves into rental accommodation – in which he or she now makes the landlord rich. Since a far better strategy than that would be to buy a smaller house, or a condominium, a VTB mortgage in fact can represent a trap. And it's one that a lot of people fall into, not least because in addition to any other factors that favor the borrower, inflation may strip the monthly payments of some value. Worse, if that money is being spent by the former owner as it comes in every month, then by the time the mortgage has been paid off, interest and principal, he's left with nothing – no house, no funds.

That's why it makes so much more sense for the seller of the house to borrow the money from the bank and re-lend it to the purchaser, who can now pay cash for the house – cash that the seller can invest in a mutual fund or a stock portfolio, for example, that will stay ahead of inflation. The purchaser is now servicing the vendor's loan.

So, except for that situation, I would generally advise the seller not to take back a first or second mortgage, unless it's the one thing that will swing the deal. And then only offer it for one year. Unlike a mortgage that's attached to an RRSP, which must fall approximately in line with the current rates available at lending institutions, a VTB mortgage can be offered at whatever rate the buyer and seller agree to. But in all cases, the vendor must look at the real cost involved, and if a $50,000 mortgage is going to effectively knock $10,000 off the price of the house, because of its lower interest rate, then he'd be better off simply reducing the price by that $10,000 and getting cash. And be done with it.

Of course, VTB mortgages, like any other investment, can subsequently be sold, and few vendors of a house will waive the right to do so. It's not a complicated transaction – often a small ad in the newspaper is enough – and if interest rates have taken a drop, a mortgage with a good yield will be easy to dispose of. But in the same way, if rates climb, then the person who decides he has to sell a VTB mortgage on the open market is probably going to take a beating, which is another reason to offer the mortgage for no longer than a year, at which time the new owner has to pay up, refinance, or give the house back. I know people, in fact, who've made a lot of money by taking their houses back when the mortgages came due, but this is a dangerous, not to say unethical, game to play because by the time the house is repossessed, it may have risen in value, but it's also liable to have been wrecked.

The "Granny" Mortgage

VTB mortgages are sometimes arranged when property changes hands within a family, or between close friends. Unfortunately, however, family loans can be among the worst forms of risk, involving late payments, a reluctance to sue, and hard feelings all round. Among a lot of new Canadians, lending money within the family is a tradition, and part of that tradition is a pride in paying it back. So if the trust and goodwill are there, it's a move that makes sense. But with one proviso: the loan should still have the same security and guarantees as any other.

With that said, the best option available, when a house is changing hands between two relatives who trust each other, is to do something that sounds like financial madness but which actually works very well – and that is to take back the mortgage interest-free. Let's say there's $60,000 involved and a father decides to lend it to his son, interest-free, spread over 10 years. With a monthly payment of $500, a total of $6,000 is repaid each year and, at the end of the term, the loan has been paid off in full. But, you say, the father has lost a fortune: 10 years' worth of interest on his money. It's certainly true that father has lost money, but look at what else has happened. Because there's no interest, the payments have been solely toward the principal: and that's tax-free income each year. In the case of a person in the 40-per-cent tax bracket, that $500 coming in every month is actually the equivalent of $700: if it was a conventional VTB mortgage, which is income like any, the taxman would be clipping $200 off it each month, assuming all other things to be equal. So the interest-free loan may not cost the lender anything at all. Meanwhile, the borrower is way, way ahead, because he's escaping the burden of a normal mortgage, which as we know can end up costing 3 or 4 times its face value. If a father lends his son the money on that basis, and the mortgage is paid off by the end of the 10-year term, it has effectively put the son 15 years ahead of his peers.

And if the son is a decent sort, he might at that point say to his father: "Thanks. Now we're going to give you something in return, for your retirement.'' Perhaps the interest-free mortgage has allowed him to buy a house that's big enough to contain an in-laws' suite, in which the parents could live rent-free. Not a bad deal for the son, considering he's been saved 15 years' worth of mortgage payments. And meanwhile, of course, the house will have risen in value. This arrangement, which I affectionately call the ''Granny'' Mortgage, can obviously be applied to any form of loan – there doesn't have to be a granny, or a mortgage, or even a piece of real estate. For everyone's sake, draw up a legal agreement, perhaps containing a clause to the effect that interest will begin to accrue in the event of the borrower falling behind in his payments. Of course, any plans for a ''gift'' to the father – or whoever the benefactor is – cannot be part of the written agreement because, if it is, Revenue Canada will regard the gift as a form of interest. This arrangement, therefore, has to be an understanding; hence the need for complete trust on both sides.

But the money for that ''gift'' has to come from somewhere, you say. Right. And here's where: take that same situation of a house that the father wants to sell to his son, for which a $60,000 mortgage is required. First, work out what an interest-free loan will save the son each month. In our case, a conventional 10-per-cent mortgage amortized over 10 years would require him to make monthly payments to the bank of $850.82, and, over the lifetime of the mortgage, that $60,000 loan would actually cost a total of $185,000. Meanwhile, father works out what his $60,000 would be doing for him if the money were invested in a savings account at 6 1/2 per cent. He discovers that after taxes were paid it would have amounted to $117,000. That's quite a loss, he thinks. However, the son has had an idea. What if he were to obtain the zero-interest loan from father – $500 a month – take the difference between what he's paying and what he WOULD be paying to the bank – $350.82 a month – and put it in a savings account. Some people would be more ambitious, but the son, like his father, is a cautious type. Every month he faithfully sends father his non-taxable $500, while at the same time socking $350 away into the same modest 6-1/2-per-cent savings account, where it steadily grows over the next 10 years. Similarly, the father takes his $500 cheque each month and puts that into a 6-1/2-per-cent daily savings account. In both cases, income tax is paid on those earnings every year, of course (and there's no longer the $1,000 exemption), but nonetheless, by the time the zero-interest mortgage is paid off, see what's happened to both bank accounts. In the case of the son, the monthly $350 contributions have compounded into an after-tax total of more than $55,000, while father's accumulated interest equals $18,000. Now, what if the son were to then give his father that $55,000 and wipe the slate clean? Here's what has happened now with our zero-interest free mortgage: the father has gotten his $60,000 back, interest-free, plus $18,000, plus $55,000 – a total of $133,000, as against the $117,000 he would have earned. The son, meanwhile, has parted with $60,000 plus the $55,000 – $115,000 as opposed to the $185,000 the conventional mortgage would have cost. Rather than giving all of the $55,000 to the father, the son might want to tilt things a little more in his own favor – but whatever the divvying-up, the theory remains the same: the lower the interest rate on a mortgage, the more money is actually applied to the principal. And in this case, by circumventing the bank, the $70,000 the son has saved would all have been in interest payments: he's escaped the burden of the amortization schedule. The no-interest mortgage is the most damatic example of these savings, but the same idea holds true of any loan that is given at below the market rate.

Remember, however, that if a father in the 40-per-cent tax bracket lends his son money at 6 per cent, instead of putting it in the bank at the going rate of 10 per cent, he's going to be out of pocket. He might figure that he would in any case lose that 4-per-cent differential, because he'd pay it out in income tax, but what he overlooks is the fact that he'll still have to pay 40-per-cent tax on the 6-per-cent yield, and he'll end up with a 3.6-per-cent net gain. So in this case, it's only the son who has come out ahead.

Many families, of course, lend money to Junior and never report that income. But by not doing so, it's worth restating, they're guilty of tax evasion. In his tax-reform program, Mr. Wilson made it clear that Ottawa will be seeking stiffer penalties for tax dodgers and perpetrators of (in his words) "artificial tax-avoidance transactions." Back in 1979, when Joe Clark promised us tax-deductible mortgages, it was generally believed that doing so would turn out to be a tremendous windfall for Revenue Canada because it would then be able to cross-refer and see whether all the lenders were paying tax on the interest they were getting. By not allowing tax-deductible mortgages some people say Revenue Canada is actually losing money overall – by not being able to catch the cheaters.

The other situation worth noting here is that of the individual who doesn't have a 25-per-cent down payment on a house and hence has to get NHA insurance on the loan, which can be up to 2 per cent tacked on to the mortgage, amortized over the life of the mortgage. In this case, it's often well worth borrowing the shortfall from a relative to get inside that 25-per-cent ballpark, and then subsequently taking out a small second mortgage to pay off the relative.

A person offered a VTB is usually being offered a better

deal than that available from the bank, both in the rate, and the prepayment privileges – but there can be all kinds of variables included. A useful addendum for the buyer can be the right to guaranteed renewal, a handy proviso to be able to fall back on if interest rates look like they might take a jump. When rates were at 18 per cent, I once got a 1-year 12-per-cent mortgage with the right to renew it at 10 per cent. The sellers didn't particularly like that, of course, but it was the condition that enabled them to sell the house – and, in turn, to buy another depressed-price property. In the same way, a seller may try to write that renewal option into the agreement, which is something the purchaser should be extremely wary of. Another term that can sometimes be negotiated is for the VTB mortgage to be compounded annually, as opposed to semiannually.

One thing for the buyer to watch out for is any clause in the agreement whereby missing a payment automatically creates a default and makes the mortgage come due. With a conventional loan, the borrower generally has a lot more grace. Another unpleasant feature (for the buyer) can be a clause requiring a nonrefundable down payment toward the VTB mortgage itself (which the vendor keeps, if for some reason the deal collapses). If such a down payment is asked for, a buyer should make sure that, like the down payment on the house itself, it bears interest.

Investing in Mortgages

It's remarkable – and unfortunate – how many people, particularly those nearing retirement, sell off their house and move into a rental unit, deciding that they'll sink their money into term deposits or GICs, and live off the proceeds. One of the problems here is that these rarely yield a monthly income, which people in this position very often want. The other drawback is that the money is generally locked in. Mutual funds, by contrast, offer a systematic withdrawal plan, whereby you get back a "mix" of money, which is taxed at a lower rate, and that happens to be my favorite choice.

One aspect of the mortgage, however, is that in addition to a "blended" monthly income (so that only a part of it is taxable), you also have a call on the house. As well, if you want to, you can always sell the mortgage. And the person who has lent out money when rates were high is likely to find that mortgage an extremely salable item in the event that rates come down.

What about the drawbacks? They can be reduced to one word: the risk. Your mortgage is not insured by Ottawa, whereas the term deposit you may have your eye on is. Neither is there the professional money management that you get with a mutual fund. If the person doesn't make his payments, you have to sue him. Granted, if you sue and win, you get the house back, but as we've noted earlier, it may be in less than perfect condition, especially if there was a very small down payment. And maybe you now want to resell. If so, you'll find that an empty house is harder to sell than an occupied one. Or what about the mortgagor who's just late with his payments – every month? That can be a major headache. And there's something else. That "blended" payment of interest and principal that arrives in the mail each month is good from a tax standpoint, but don't forget that at the end of the term there's nothing left. Which is fine if you've been reinvesting that income, but if you've just been living off it, there's not going to be anything left. And it's amazing how many people don't take account of that fact.

For an older person who really does want to live in rented accommodation, or who perhaps just wants to buy and live in a smaller house, my preference would be to see her invest in a mutual fund, which a) offers a systematic withdrawal plan, b) is almost tax-free, and c) allows her investment to rise in value. In many ways, the mutual fund offers the best of all possible worlds.

Chapter 8

Breaking a Mortgage

Closed mortgages are much less common than they used to be, and for the borrower that's good news because the only consolation to being locked into one is that the interest rate will likely be marginally lower than if there is an escape hatch. Taking into account the different options that become available in opening up, or breaking, a mortgage, that half-a-per-cent or 1-per-cent saving is rarely worth it, unless of course interest rates start heading for the roof. In the same way, a borrower pays top dollar for a fully open mortgage, which can be broken at any time without penalty. That's if he can get one: they're a rarity with the major lending institutions.

All mortgages become fully open on maturity, but until that date, a closed mortgage means exactly that. There's a myth that any mortgage can automatically be disposed of by paying a penalty of 3 months' interest. Not so. The Mortgages Act does specify that after 5 years any residential mortgage can be redeemed with a maximum 3-month penalty (this doesn't apply in the case of a mortgage issued by a joint stock company or other corporation), and with a National Housing Association mortgage, insured by the Canada Mortgage Housing Corporation, it's 3 years. However, a clause allowing the borrower to break it before then, or to make a partial prepayment, is still a "privilege." As well, some mortgages are divided into two component parts, one of which – typically 10 per cent per year – can be paid down while the other remains closed. In other cases, the mortgage comes open (on payment of the penalty) after a specified period of time has elapsed. A borrower should therefore not assume that paying 3 months' interest will get him off the hook; anyone who breaks a closed mortgage has broken an agreement, and can be sued, creating long-term problems for his credit rating.

Happily, the fierce competition between lending institutions has meant that – for a price – most mortgages can be opened up. Far from damaging your credit rating, breaking a mortgage in this way is playing ball with the lender, and the question is therefore simply whether the price tag is worth it. With a 3-month penalty, it often is, but a rate-differential clause, which becomes common when interest rates are volatile, is a different story. The differential will be worked out on the basis of the lifetime of the mortgage and, in general, if there is a differential cost instead of a 3-month penalty, it won't be worthwhile to break the mortgage. Why? Because the more attractive a new, low-cost loan looks, the bigger the spread is between the two rates and the more it's going to cost to get out of the old one.

There's another variable the borrower should be aware of with a rate-differential. The lump sum payment in this situation is obviously a windfall to the lender because he can then immediately relend that money to someone else: he is, in effect, getting the use of it twice. Some institutions will take account of this and compensate the borrower through reducing the penalty by what's called a "current value adjustment," which gives back to the borrower some of the lender's windfall. In the case of a 25-year-amortized $50,000 mortgage, being refinanced because interest rates have fallen from 16 per cent to 12, the roughly $4,000 that it would cost to break the mortgage would be reduced by about $700 through applying "current value adjustment." Even in this case, however, the net cost of making the rate-differential kick in is still likely to outweigh the benefits. In fact, there are still people locked into loans in which the only way out is the 3-month penalty PLUS the differential – a deadly situation. So when you negotiate the loan, be sure to assess the cost of getting out.

There's a formula to apply. Let's say you have exactly 3 years of a mortgage left to run – 36 monthly payments. Add them up, then go to the lender and find out – to the penny – what it will cost you to cancel the loan. And then, work out what it will cost to renew the mortgage at current rates, whether from that lender or from another one. Take into account the new monthly payment levels, the penalty, if there is one, plus any fees for the paperwork. Balance the two sets of figures together and, if you'll be better off breaking the mortgage and paying the penalty, break it.

The savings can be considerable. Say interest rates have fallen 3 percentage points since the time you signed the mortgage papers, dropping from 13 1/2 per cent to 10 1/2. As things stand, you have $65,000 outstanding on a loan amortized over 25 years, and every month you service it with a payment of $739.73 – a total of $26,630.28 after the 3 years. With a 10-1/2-per-cent loan, there's a monthly payment of $603.42, so you'll have parted with $21,723.12 at the end of the same period. Add this to the 3-month penalty and you have your total. Even allowing for any administrative costs, you're still more than $3,000 ahead by breaking the mortgage.

But that's just the interest. That calculation shows you what you've saved in terms of cash in your pocket, but when the 3 years is up and it's time to renew the mortgage again, see what's happened in the meantime to the principal, with payments based on the lower rate. You can be certain that it will be less than with the old mortgage because the lower the interest rate, the higher the percentage of each monthly payment going toward the principal – even though you have been writing out a smaller cheque each month. Again, just add the figures. Assuming that in both cases there is exactly $65,000 owing, in the case of the 13-1/2-per-cent loan the outstanding balance after 3 years' payments is $63,765. In the case of the 10-1/2-per-cent mortgage, the balance will have fallen to $63,050 – a $715 saving. Spread over the remaining 22 years of the mortgage at 10 1/2 per cent, it would be worth $1,752.

This is comparing apples to apples – two 36-month mortgages, which is a more useful way of assessing real costs than weighing the price of breaking the first mortgage against the expense of, say, a series of low-interest 6-month loans, which will contain their own costs. However, if interest rates look like they're going to come down – and you're a gambler – the 6-month mortgage can save you a lot of money. If the rates are falling, all the more reason to get out of a high-cost mortgage. It might be tempting to wait until they've bottomed out, but that can be an expensive wait and, in this case, a short-term interim loan can be a good idea until things have stabilized.

The variable mortgage is almost always open, on payment of a penalty. The interest rate, at the outset, tends to be lower than the conventional going rate and, if you have a variable mortgage, clearly you want to stick with it as long as interest rates are falling. When it was costing 18 and 20 per cent to borrow, anyone who got a variable-rate mortgage was in great shape, it subsequently turned out, because when the rates crumbled, monthly payments plummeted as well. If rates look like they're going to rise, switch over and lock into a conventional mortgage. A variable-rate mortgage can represent a real gamble because although the rate itself floats, moving up or down each month in lockstep with the prime bank rate, the actual monthly payment is generally fixed for the lifetime of the mortgage. Whether the rate goes up or down, the payment is the same and, then, when the mortgage comes due, there is either a credit or a debit. If rates go through the roof, a borrower may owe more at the end of the term than he did at the beginning.

As we've said, a closed mortgage means exactly that, but there's often room for negotiation – the lender may be amenable to settling up for a few months' worth of interest. For the borrower who wants to do better than that, and who's got lots of nerve, a device that's been used as a means of getting out from under a closed mortgage is "intentional default," whereby he ceases making payments and the lender commences foreclosure or power-of-sale proceedings. What this does – by law – is automatically open up the mortgage for prepayment, and the borrower's only costs are the arrears and his and the lender's legal expenses. And then he can go elsewhere for new financing. Great trick if you can get away with it, but also a very dangerous one, not only because of severe damage to one's credit rating, but also because the lender will probably decide to simply sue for the backpayments, rather than foreclosing. There may be double trouble in store if you have a second mortgage on the house, and the second mortgagee finds out you're being sued on the first one – because there's a good chance he has a clause in the agreement stating that if the first mortgage is in trouble, he gets first crack at taking it over. (Similarly, some second or third residential mortgages contain a clause to the effect that when the first mortgage comes due, the second mortgagee has first right to renewal, which is something else the borrower should steer away from.)

In Alberta, in recent years, after energy prices went through the floor, breaking mortgages and abandoning houses became quite common, and for people in a squeeze it was often a move that made sense. The difference between intentional default, as outlined above, and simply dropping the house keys on the banker's desk and walking away is that in the second case the house is being given back. In theory, the bank still had the right to sue those Albertans because an agreement had been broken, but in fact this rarely happened. The bank had its collateral, and the fact that it couldn't subsequently unload the property was not the borrower's problem. In fact, it often wasn't the bank's problem either, because many of those houses in Calgary and Edmonton had NHA insurance on them, so in the end it was the taxpayer who picked up the loss. Most of those people who broke their mortgages ended up better off, even though they'd lost their equity: they'd gotten out from under a market that was in a severe slump and were now free to buy another house that was similar to the one they'd left behind, but a great deal less expensive. Those people's credit ratings may not have been improved, but they were not damaged like that of the mortgagor who stops making payments and says to the lender: "Force me out." Even where there's a negative credit rating, most lenders will still do business, although they'll be almost certain to insist that NHA insurance is put on the property.

Foreclosure is different. You may owe not just for arrears and legal bills, but also for any losses when the house is sold. If there are problems on the horizon, far better to go to the lender, right off the bat, because there are things that can be done. And the bigger the mortgage, the better the chance of you controlling the banker rather than the other way round. Look at Brazil: effectively, it owns the banks because the banks can't afford to foreclose.

Finally – and as always – a forced savings plan works wonders. If you've broken the mortgage, renegotiated the financing, and replaced a $500 monthly payment with a $400 one, keep on paying $500, salt away the extra $100, and use it to pay down the principal.

Chapter 9

Weekly and Long-Term Mortgages

Weekly Mortgages

Up until a few years ago, a mortgage generally meant a monthly mortgage, although some credit unions have always offered weekly mortgages. But then came the time when nobody wanted to borrow any money because interest rates had gone through the ceiling, and this prompted the banks to open up their marketing with all kinds of bells and whistles. In the case of mortgages, the result of the new competition has meant greater flexibility in the type of loan and in the prepayment rules. That's certainly good news for the borrower because years can be knocked off the lifetime of the loan – but if she plays her cards right, she can do better still.

123

There are two types of weekly mortgages and, as a device for reducing the principal, one is much more effective than the other. The first involves simply computing the annual amount of money that would be paid out through 12 conventional payments, dividing the total into 52, and writing a weekly cheque for that amount. At the end of the year, the borrower will have parted with an identical sum of money as he would have with a standard mortgage, but, at the same time, there will have been a slight daisy-chain effect on the principal: the weekly payments will have been chipping away at that money a little faster than monthly payments would have done. The result? Over the lifetime of a $50,000 mortgage, amortized over 25 years at a relatively high 13 per cent, about $4,500 would have been knocked off the approximately $115,500 worth of interest, while the 25-year term would be reduced by 8 months. No big deal, but still a useful saving, and the higher the rates, the bigger the dent in the principal. If it's a $60,000 loan at 10 per cent, there'd be a net saving of only $3,491, while shaving 6 months off the life of the loan.

So that's well worth doing – ANYTHING that eases the sting of amortization is worth doing – but it's the second type of mortgage that has become popular because, in this case, the benefits can be really substantial. This essentially involves making 13 monthly payments per year, instead of 12. For the bank, all that's involved is some extra paperwork, while for the borrower it represents a very powerful method of forced savings. Fine – but with a little extra footwork, you can do better still and, in fact, if you play your cards right, you don't need a weekly mortgage from the bank at all. Here's why.

Going back to our example of a $60,000 mortgage at 10 per cent, the normal monthly payment would be $536.69 a month – that's a calendar month, remember – which adds up to $6,440.20 per year. The way a weekly mortgage schedule would normally work in this case would be for the borrower to divide the $536.60 into four components of $134.17 and write out a cheque for that much every week of the year. At the end of year, he's parted with 52 times $134.17, which comes to $6,976.50. In effect, 13 payments have been made, instead of 12. Doing things that way will save the borrower $30,663 in total interest and reduce the lifetime of the mortgage to 18.7 years. If, on top of that, he pays down the mortgage every year to the tune of an extra $1,000, which most lending institutions will let you do, then such is the accumulative damage to the principal that in this case a 25-year mortgage gets paid off in under 14 years, with a total saving of $51,537.

Great going – and that's exactly the reason you don't need a weekly mortgage from the bank and, in fact, would do better to stick with a monthly mortgage and superimpose your own schedule of weekly payments. Simply take the current monthly payment, multiply it by 13, and you have the equivalent of a weekly mortgage. There are at least two reasons to do this. The first saving is in the fee that may be asked for administering a weekly mortgage, but, more important, consider what would happen if you were to turn things around and make that extra 13th payment at the BEGINNING of the year, instead of at the end. We've already noted the daisy-chain effect of weekly payments, but, in this case, making that $536 payment in January instead of in December will put the money to work for the whole year. Do THAT every year, and you'll wipe another whole year off the mortgage. That's right and, in our chapter on amortization, we'll look more closely at the mechanics of how this works.

There's another trap with conventional weekly mortgages

and, where it exists, it's a third reason to do things yourself. Some lenders have gotten into the practice of compounding – or "adjusting" – mortgages more often than twice a year. The standard wording on a mortgage contract calls for the interest on the loan to be adjusted "semiannually, not in advance." But with weekly mortgages, some lenders want more than that. If a person has money deposited in a savings account, then the more frequently the interest is compounded, the better it is for the depositor – hence the flurry of advertisements for daily interest accounts. With a mortgage, it's the same thing in reverse – the borrower is paying interest on interest. And if your mortgage is being compounded once a month instead of once every 6 months, then look out: the result can add up to a full year's extra payments. You might not care about that. You may say: "With a weekly mortgage, I'm still paying the thing off in 14 years instead of 25. I've saved tens of thousands of dollars in interest." True enough, but had you done things my way, you could have paid it off in 13 years.

For the same reason, it's well worth trying to negotiate over the mortgage-compounding, something that a private lender may well agree to discuss, particularly in the case of a vendor-take-back mortgage. In my own case once, when I was paying a vendor-take-back mortgage, I demanded annual compounding, and got it. The frequency with which the interest on a loan gets compounded can be either a plus or a minus, and it's a factor that tends to get overlooked.

There are all kinds of variations on the weekly mortgage – biweekly, for instance, and semimonthly, together with a range of prepayment variables – but a lot of people like weekly mortgages because they get a weekly paycheque. And while a bimonthly mortgage will be paid off faster than a monthly one, and a weekly one more quickly than a bimonthly one, the logic is the same: you will accelerate the prepayment process by organizing it yourself and applying the extra money at the beginning of the year instead of at the end.

Some homeowners who become aware of the accumulative force that goes to work with a rigorous prepayment schedule contemplate breaking their mortgage so as to refinance on a weekly basis. This makes little sense if there's a 3-month penalty attached to the mortgage. Far better to take the money you would forfeit and put it directly against the principal.

In the same way, a person who's locked into a high-interest mortgage at a time when rates are relatively low should consider borrowing some extra cash simply to make an extra payment against the principal – even if it's just the $500 or $600 that is the equivalent of a 13th payment. Deciding whether to use a short-term loan to knock a hole in a long-term debt becomes a matter of straight arithmetic, and we'll examine that more closely in the amortization chapter as well.

This is why it's so important, when financing or refinancing, to examine the prepayment privileges. Because of the competition between the major lending institutions in the past 2 or 3 years, most mortgages allow the borrower to either make an extra payment or pay down 10 per cent of the principal, and sometimes they'll do even better. At the time of writing, many of the Big Five banks were letting customers increase their monthly payment by 20 per cent and also pay 20 per cent against the principal any time they wished – rather than just on the anniversary date. And the best thing for those customers to have done, if they possibly could, was both.

Long-Term Mortgages

Despite the recent popularity of short-term mortgages, long-term loans – for 7 years, 10 years, or even more – are likely to become a permanent part of the scenery once again. One of the key developments here has been the advent of mortgage-backed securities. These are investment vehicles that trade in the money markets and are underpinned by residential mortgages insured by The Canada Mortgage and Housing Corporation. With that security built in, these "Cannie Maes," as they've been dubbed (after their U.S. counterparts, known as "Ginnie Maes"), allow a financial institution to borrow money for a longer period of time, meaning that the institution, in turn, can then lend it out to consumers for a longer term, safe in the knowledge that the interest rate is fixed. Some economists predict that the long-term result will be lower interest rates: more money available for mortgage financing will increase the competition among lenders. In the meantime, however, the question is: is a long-term loan something the borrower wants? In times of rising rates, of course, it is – he wants that money locked away – and so this is a situation where a little research before taking on that loan will go a long way. If analysts are saying rates are going to move up for the next 2 years, a 3-year fixed mortgage probably looks good. And vice versa if they look like they're coming down, when a short-term loan or, better still, a variable-rate loan is what you want. I know of one family, in fact, who took a variable-rate mortgage in 1981 and rode the thing right down to bottom, paying off the entire mortgage in 5 years without making a single additional payment.

A short-term mortgage is almost invariably cheaper than a long-term loan, of course, reflecting the EXISTING cost of money, as opposed to the possible future cost, which is what the lender has to budget for. And in return, the borrower is at the mercy of the marketplace, 6 months or a year down the road. Picking the term is therefore always a gamble, in which security is balanced against short-term gains. In general – writing in early 1991 – I can't imagine locking into a 7- or 10-year mortgage, especially when interest rates have edged up a point or two in the last year. Why? Because the additional cost of the mortgage would be disproportionately high. In a recession, interest rates always fall.

We've been talking so far about the individual who's still got a long way to go before the house is paid off. But in the case of a homeowner who's down to the last 7 years or so on his mortgage, and who just doesn't want to play this guessing game any more, I could make a pretty good case for a 7-year mortgage. Because for that person the worst that could happen would be that rates were to fall. Ten years? I think that's too long for any mortgage: the spread in the rates will be too wide and there'll be too little room to maneuver. Far better to lock into a fixed, 3-year loan – and opt for every possible prepayment privilege. If you're a first-time home buyer, with a small amount of equity and everything on the line, maybe you'd want to make that 5 years – that way you know you can deal with any headaches along the way – but don't forget: the longer the term of the loan, the more important it is to make prepayments. The other thing to be taken into account is job security, and the prospect of any increased income. If there is an extra chunk of cash coming in, then a buyer has an edge that he can use to gamble a little: he knows that by taking that extra money and applying it to the principal he will probably be able to offset any increase in the rates.

I think it's likely we'll see the return of the 25-year mortgage – amortized for that period of time and with a fixed interest rate. But as a rule, we can say that the more equity you have in your home, the more you should think in terms of playing the short-term market, especially if you have an investment or two to back you up. In the case of the homeowner who has paid off the house and who now borrows against it to buy investments, he should generally think short-term rather than long-term because he wants the flexibility that will allow him to cash in the investments and settle up. And, in fact, a plain demand loan may be the best bet in this case, despite its higher price tag.

Most mortgages in Canada are amortized for up to 25 years, but what about the buyer who's tempted to stretch that up to 30 or 35 years, thereby lowering the mortgage payment? I can think of two words to describe that scenario: licensed thievery. It became common to do this when rates were very high because it enabled the lender to say: "Well, you don't quite fit our criteria. However, with a 30-year loan, the payments will be less, and you qualify." But look at the difference in cost! The monthly cost is a few bucks less, meanwhile adding another 60 payments to the mortgage. In the case of a $50,000 loan at 10 per cent, 25-year amortization has a monthly payment of

$447.25. Increase the mortgage to 35 years and the figure is $431.34. The borrower is saving less than $16 a month – $4 a week – while, in the meantime, the overall cost of the mortgage has soared by more than $11,000. Tell your enemies to amortize their mortgages over 30 years. We'll examine this in detail a little later on.

Chapter 10

Borrowing Against Your House

When you go to a lender to borrow money against your house - for whatever reason - he's going to be looking at more than the fact that you have some equity in a chunk of real estate. The classic situation, and I've known it to happen, is when a person owns a half-million-dollar house and he's out of work. Everything's crumbled around him and all he has is this beautiful asset. Great collateral. Now how is he going to make the monthly payments? The trouble is the banker's not in the business of bankruptcy, repossession, selling houses, etc.; he's in the business of lending money - and he knows more about it than you do about borrowing money. His concern is really quite simple: are the payments going to be made on time? And that's certainly the thing that his superiors want to know about. So for the same reason, he might be prepared to lend money with little or no collateral, if he can be convinced that his cheque is going to arrive every month.

Most homeowners, however, have a bit of both - equity and enough of an income to service the loan - and, with that, they should be able to go into the bank from a position of strength: you've been faithfully paying down the mortgage, meanwhile watching the house rise in value, and now it's time to make that built-up equity go to work. When you do decide to make a move, the key thing is to have mapped out a strategy. When you go to the Grey Cup, or the Superbowl, do you think they suddenly make up the plays in the huddle? It's the same thing. You have to present the lender with a clear, concise, businesslike plan, because if you're not sure, he won't be sure - and he's not sure anyway.

And so right off, he'll want to know what your assets are, and your liabilities. Best of all is if you can say: "My salary is enough to pay off the loan without you needing to have any collateral." If you're asking $8,000 a year more than you need and want to borrow $50,000 at 12 per cent, that'll require annual payments of $6,000. In this instance, the banker can see that you've got 33 per cent more than is required to service the loan and he'll almost certainly be willing to lend the money on a straight cash flow. And the purpose of the loan makes a big difference, too. In the case of our $50,000, you already have sufficient excess monthly income to cover the payments, but if you're borrowing to invest in a rental property that will not only yield an income to help service the loan, but also create tax deductions - so much the better. And while there are certain assets - such as RRSPs - that can't be taken as collateral, they CAN be taken into consideration. If they're on deposit at the bank, they can be monitored as an indication of your financial stability. That's the kind of thing that has to be clear in your own mind in order to demonstrate that basically you don't need the money. The old definition of a bank used to be that on a sunny day it'll give you an umbrella, but, as soon as it rains, it'll yank it away from you.

Since the lender will undoubtedly be in touch with the local credit bureau, it's never a bad idea to pay a visit yourself to try to find out what they have on file. I once found myself receiving enormous hydro bills, which I was naturally rather reluctant to pay. In making inquiries, I learned from the hydro company that this was because I was the "owner" of a duplex across the street – and, in fact, the hydro company had a letter from a lawyer telling them so. Finding the real owner wasn't hard – I put the house up for sale, and he emerged from the woodwork rather swiftly – and it was at that point that we discovered there were two Brian Costellos! Mistakes can, and do, happen, and clearing up any problems BEFORE the lender contacts the credit bureau is obviously a good idea, especially if it helps the borrower get a better interest rate, which will generally be the case if he can obtain a demand loan as opposed to a conventional mortgage.

People are often nervous about putting up their home as collateral for a loan, but their thinking here is sometimes muddled. If you decide to put up stocks and bonds as security, and the project goes bad and you can't pay up, then if the loss is greater than the collateral do you think the lender won't come after the house anyway? Of course he will, and what he'll do, in that case, is possess it, recoup his loss, and give you whatever's left over. If you don't want to put up your house as collateral, then whatever it is that you do offer will have to have a solid – and easily verifiable – track record. But, in a sense, it doesn't matter whether you put up the house as security or not: if things come to the crunch, that's what you'll have to fall back on in any case.

It's clearly a bad idea to put a mortgage out on a home to borrow for something that's highly speculative, and if you can't service the loan on your EXISTING income, then don't borrow. Borrowing to invest in a business is a slightly different story if the business is incorporated, because if it's incorporated, then the losses won't be any greater than the business assets, and the house is safe. Needless to say, the banker is not stupid, so if the venture looks dicey, he's going to ask for your personal covenant. If that's the case, then further on down the road, when the investment has grown and prospered, the borrower should renegotiate and seek to have that provision removed. And if the assets are now there, the lender should be amenable. Remember the bank doesn't really WANT your house. What it wants is to know that its loan is secure.

What if you borrow against your house and then, maybe a few months later, circumstances change and you want to refinance? We've already looked at the pros and cons of breaking a mortgage and a basic rule, we know, is that if interest rates are rising, we lock the loan in, if only for one or two years. If they're falling, we go for a variable-rate loan. But a loan doesn't have to be a mortgage per se – a demand loan becomes a mortgage if you've put up your house as collateral. And, in fact, there are good reasons why a demand loan – which the lender can call whenever he wants, i.e., in the event of payments not being made – is a better deal for the borrower. It's instantly negotiable; it can be transferred from bank to bank; and it's cheaper to put in place because there are usually no legal fees, no appraisal, no insurance fees. The potential disadvantage of the demand loan is that it's in lockstep with the prime lending rate, following it automatically up or down, which is fine as long as rates are falling. In fact, I know of people who took out a variable-rate mortgage in 1981 and paid off the whole thing in 5 years without increasing their payments at all, just because interest rates fell so dramatically. Look at where all their peers are; they've still got 20 years to go. But of course, things can go the other way. With a demand loan, remember, you HAVE to make your payments, and the bank won't show the same reluctance to foreclose that it will with a conventional mortgage. But the great thing about it is its flexibility.

When a mortgage is due and a homeowner has a number of debts outstanding, it's sometimes tempting to refinance by means of a package that wipes out all the smaller debts and rolls everything into one "convenient" payment. This may seem like an especially good idea if rates have come down, and indeed, as long as the house has risen in value, the lender will probably be willing to go along with it. But you have to remember that by doing things that way you're now amortizing that 3-year car loan, or credit card payment, over anything up to 25 years. The net cost may be substantially higher in the end than it would otherwise have been. One useful ploy in this situation is to consolidate all the debts, taking advantage of the lower rate, but to increase the ACTUAL payment, thereby paying off more of the principal and shortening the amortization period.

Something else to beware of in refinancing is the "wrap-around" mortgage in which a lender takes over an existing low-cost mortgage and provides a new, larger one. Even though the interest on the new mortgage may in fact be lower than the going rate, the arrangement will still cost the borrower money if the net result is to increase the cost on the original loan. If you want to borrow $50,000 and currently owe $50,000 on a 10-per-cent loan, then a renegotiated loan for $100,000 at 15 per cent might look like a great idea if rates have zoomed to 18 per cent. In fact, you would be worse off because the 5-point spread between the 10- and 15-per-cent rates will more than wipe out the 3-per-cent difference between the 15- and the 18-per-cent rate.

If you're planning to lodge your house as collateral for a loan, don't waste money on getting it formally appraised, which homeowners sometimes do so they can go into the bank better armed. Instead, call in a real estate agent, or a couple of them, and ask them what they'd list the property for. Whatever the figure, the bank will generally go along with it because the bank knows that real estate agents tend to list on the low side as a means of luring prospective buyers. And if the bank DOES want a formal appraisal, it will have its own done – and charge you for it – so there's no point in duplicating it.

Shop around. The advantage of staying with your friendly neighborhood banker is that he's likely to offer the path of least resistance, but personally I never deal with one bank exclusively – far better to play one against the other. And for God's sake, negotiate! All the banks are selling is a product, which happens to be money, and when you walk through those big marble pillars it's easy to forget they want your business. If they weren't, why would they advertise? The same holds true of all the other lenders. So if you have an insurance policy with Sun Life, for example, why not ask it about a mortgage, too? Incidentally, for people who took out insurance policies before 1967, and which were cash-value policies (meaning they have investments attached), there is an option allowing the money in the policy to be borrowed at a maximum of 6 per cent. But even with policies taken out after that date, money can still often be borrowed at a better rate than is available from the bank. Credit unions attached to the company where you work are another source of cheaper money. And whatever the institution, one small but often overlooked detail is that if you don't know the person behind the desk, get a reference from someone who already deals there, rather than going in cold.

Don't borrow more than you can afford to pay back and don't borrow to go into something speculative – that's not investing, that's gambling. But one difference between borrowing against your house and using, say, stocks as collateral, or a business, is that if property values take a dive, the bank is still unlikely to call the loan – even though its security may now be less – as long as the payments are made. If stocks or mutual funds take a tumble, on the other hand, the lender is likely to be more nervous and can give what's termed a margin call, as we discussed in the chapter on making a mortgage tax-deductible. With a house as collateral in a depressed market, lending institutions shy away from putting a gun to the borrower's head because they have the security of knowing that, in the long term, property values head in one direction, and one direction alone.

What about borrowing against your house to buy a weekend cottage, or a property that's not normally considered a rental operation? The first thing is that the interest on the loan for what will be regarded as a second home is not going to be tax-deductible. So if it's in any way possible – and unlike the purchase of a house for which the interest is deductible – buy it outright. Pay cash. If there isn't enough cash around, but there are investments available, then consider selling them to get that cash. And then – bearing in mind, of course, the proviso we discussed at the beginning of the book – buy them back.

Chapter 11

Insurance and Property Taxes

Fire/Theft/Damage Insurance

A piece of real estate is probably the most expensive purchase you'll ever make, and whether you think it needs to be insured or not, any lender will insist that it be insured. But where a lot of people go wrong is in saying: "I've bought this $100,000 house, therefore I need $100,000 worth of insurance." That's usually not true. Now, there are situations in which the house is going to be worth more than the land, but most of the time it's the other way round. Why insure the land? I've talked to lots of firemen, and they say they never lose a basement; the land doesn't burn. So don't overinsure, and the simple way to avoid doing so is with an up-to-date assessment of the land value itself. Sometimes a homeowner will take out a big insurance policy because he wants to be covered in the

141

event that property prices move up. Fine, but remember
that if the thing burns down, or is damaged by fire, or
vandals, or a flood, the insurance company is only going
to pay what it has to. You should be thinking along the
same lines; huge overinsurance is a straight waste of
money.

Sometimes a lender will demand that the fire insurance
on a house be equal to the value of the mortgage. The supposed logic here is: "If the house burns down and you
haven't got enough money to replace it, how do we know
you're going to make the payments?" Well, that's why
he's getting interest on the loan – because he's taken a
risk – and, in fact, there is no good reason for the lender
to demand that you insure for more than the value of the
bricks and mortar. The amount for which you insure the
contents of the house is your choice, and so too should be
the amount for which you insure the property. If the
lender demands more than replacement value, simply say:
"Look, I'm putting on an inflation-adjusted policy – the
insurance company's commitment is to replace the house
at current value, not depreciated value. The house is rising
in value and, meanwhile, the loan from you is shrinking
because I'm paying it down, interest and principal." If
there are outbuildings on the property, separated from
each other, that's another reason why you shouldn't be
paying insurance on both the land and the buildings
because if one structure burns down, it's not going to take
the other one with it. Remember: since the lender is almost
undoubtedly named as beneficiary in the insurance policy,
he's doing very well out of all this, most of all in a strong
real estate market, in which the value of his collateral is increasing. Don't be shy about pointing this out.

Equally, of course, it's a mistake to be underinsured.
This happens when people either 1) pay the minimum

they can get away with, to satisfy the mortgagee; or, more commonly, 2) insure the house for what they paid for it. Granted, when house prices rise, the land is almost invariably increasing in value more than the cost of building materials. But at the same time, if you remodel your kitchen and spend $10,000 doing so, the additional premium to cover that $10,000 is pretty marginal when weighed against the possibility of losing everything in a fire and being compensated only to the tune of what you paid for the house. And that happens.

So get your property reassessed every year, as part of your fall financial planning, and keep an eye on the news. I tend to file away all kinds of newspaper clippings, magazine articles, consumer-price-index fact sheets, inflation charts, anything that'll help me keep track of the real value of my house – and of the land it's sitting on. The other thing I like to have is a few good photographs of the house, inside and out, and of its contents. After a fire or a theft, a photograph (stored in a safety-deposit box) of that almost-antique could be something you were extremely glad that you had.

Shop around for fire insurance, as it's a competitive business. However many years you've been dealing with one company, be hardheaded and get several quotes on the cost of the premiums – three at least; they cost nothing. Some people think a small company can be slow to pay up, and so they instinctively insure with one of the big guys, reasoning that they're safer. But it's the smaller firms that are often more competitive. Sometimes premiums are 5 or 10 per cent lower if the homeowner installs burglar alarms or smoke detectors, but the saving is small when balanced against the cost of the installation. Talk it all through with your insurance broker, since he's the one who will go to bat for you if there's ever a problem. But remember: the odds are high that there won't be a problem, and people sometimes forget that insurance is only there IN CASE something happens. You have to have it, but to pay inflated premiums for years on end, getting back nothing in return, is to have given your money away – and there are worthier charities than insurance mega-corporations. In the end, all the lender really wants is to know that he's covered. All you want to know is that if something happens, the money will be there to rebuild that property.

If you work out of your house, insurance costs become tax-deductible, to the extent that the house is being used as a business. Perhaps a person has a four-bedroom house and uses the fourth bedroom as an office, taking up 10 per cent of his house. Ten per cent of the heat, the hydro, property taxes, mortgage interest – and 10 per cent of the fire-insurance premium will be tax-deductible. That eases the burden a little, but, at the same time, if clients are to visit the house, the owner might want to put on a higher liability policy as a precaution against being sued over an accident. It does happen. Once again, as we've discussed, don't forget that Michael Wilson has changed the rules about home offices.

If a person buys a duplex, lives in one half, and rents out the other, then, in the same way, half the fire insurance becomes tax-deductible – or possibly more. It's often the case that the premium to insure a duplex is higher than it would be if the same building were to be used as a single-family home. If so, you can make a good case to the effect that 60 per cent of the premiums are for business purposes. The breakdown would normally be 50-50, assuming the building were divided exactly in two. But if in this situation it costs $500 to insure, whereas for a single-family unit the premium would have been $400, then you could justifiably tell Revenue Canada that $300 worth of that fee is for business purposes and $200 for personal use.

We've already discussed the individual who has some equity built up in his house and who decides to borrow against it to invest, whether in stocks and bonds, mutual funds, a rental property, or a business car. If that's what he does, then a portion of the fire-insurance premiums can be written off, and he might actually want to increase that insurance, for the same reason as with any other operating cost: a net loss becomes tax-deductible against other income. Many people fail to realize this, and say simply: "I'm not going to increase the insurance on this house. I've got enough already." Obviously the extra insurance has to be justifiable, and with Revenue Canada this can be a grey area. But what is NOT a grey area is the situation in which the institution demands that you increase your property insurance. Say you have a $200,000 house, no mortgage, and you borrow $50,000 against it for investment purposes. Because there's now, in effect, a lien on the house, the lender may well require that you upgrade your insurance – and that cost is tax-deductible. Especially if the beneficiary named is the bank.

Default Insurance

Unlike fire/theft insurance, this is not compulsory except in the case of high-ratio first mortgages, by which we mean mortgages that cover 75 per cent or more of the purchase price of a house. Since the purpose of default insurance is to act as a guarantee for the lender, it's obviously something no borrower wants to pay unless he has to. The one exception to this would be a situation in which a borrower decides to walk away from a house, perhaps because property values have slumped (such as a number of Albertans did, when the bottom of the oil and gas market fell out). In this instance, the borrower might be glad he was required to pay those default-insurance premiums, which now prevent him from getting sued by the lender, because if property values have plummeted, then the lender – who, after all is just that, a merchant of money rather than of property — very likely will sue, rather than repossess. (In Alberta, what saved a lot of individuals was the fact that many of the houses were brand-new when they were purchased and were required by law to be insured against default. So in the end it was either the Mortgage Insurance Company of Canada, or, more commonly, CMHC that picked up the tab.)

Default insurance is basically there to protect the depositor who's invested his money with the trust company or the bank, which is now lending that money out as a mortgage. Up until 1964, a buyer generally had to come up with one-third of the purchase price if he was to finance the balance with a first mortgage. The subsequent advent of high-ratio mortgages, some of which were up in the 90-per-cent range, created an instability that made a lot of people nervous. Since 1970, the rule has been that lending institutions are allowed to make first-mortgage loans for more than 75 per cent of the sale price only if the mortgage – all of the mortgage – is insured, either through Canada Mortgage and Housing Corporation or its private-sector counterpart, the Mortgage Insurance Company of Canada. The cost is paid by the borrower, and he can generally decide which of the two institutions he wants to be insured with. But that's about the only choice he does get, and in some cases a lender will require that a mortgage of less than 75 per cent be insured. The trouble is the borrower in this situation is generally so strapped for cash that the premium usually has to be tacked on to the mortgage itself – and amortized over the same period of time. And that's why, no question, it's sometimes a smart move to take out a small second mortgage, perhaps a personal loan, to avoid the cost of that insurance. But I say "sometimes." Here's why.

In the spring of 1987, CMHC, taking a cue from MICC, lowered the cost of its default-insurance premiums. The move was hailed in some quarters as a big help to the would-be homeowner trying to break into an increasingly expensive real estate market, but in fact the net benefit was marginal. The general rule of thumb is that both institutions will insure up to 90 per cent of the first $125,000 on the purchase price of a house, and then 80 per cent of the balance, PROVIDED the whole financing doesn't exceed 90 per cent of the purchase price – meaning there has to be a minimum 10-per-cent down payment. Both institutions use the same sliding scale of premiums: if more than 75 per cent of the house is financed with a first mortgage, the premium will be 1 1/4 per cent of the total mortgage (not just of the portion above 75 per cent, which is what people sometimes think). Beyond 80-per-cent financing, the premium is 2 per cent. After 85 per cent, it's 2 1/2 per cent, up to the 90-per-cent cutoff, at which point you will probably decide to keep on paying rent. And by now this is all getting pretty expensive. If you buy a $125,000 house with a 10-per-cent down payment, then the 2-1/2-per-cent premium on the balance of $112,500 will cost an extra $2,813 – and that probably gets amortized along with the rest of the mortgage because if you'd had the cash to pay for the insurance premiums, you'd have used it to increase the down payment. If the mortgage is at 10 per cent, then the monthly insurance fee will amount to approximately $25 or so – growing into $7,500 if stretched out over 25 years' worth of amortization.

That looks like bad news until you look at what can happen to the person who decides, instead, to go with two mortgages, neither of which has to be insured. With that same $125,000 house and $12,500 down payment, the bank can only, by law, loan him 75 per cent of the selling price without putting on insurance. That amounts to $93,750, leaving a shortfall of $18,750. On a good day, when the sun's shining, the absolute best deal a borrower could expect on a second mortgage like that would be 3 points above the 10-1/2-per-cent rate on the first mortgage. In addition to that, there will likely be a mortgage broker's fee of several hundred dollars. Borrowing that $18,750 at 13 1/2 per cent, with the loan amortized over 25 years, calls for a monthly payment of about $212: over 25 years that's about $63,600 – nearly half again what the purchaser started out trying to borrow! He would have been vastly better off paying the insurance premium for a single, high-ratio mortgage.

This is because both the above scenarios involve the deadly business of paying out the extra money over 25 years. So the trick here therefore is – in time-honored tradition – to scrape together as big a down payment as possible WITHOUT mortgaging the extra funds, i.e., pooling whatever resources are available and perhaps supplementing them with a short-term family loan. All too frequently, however, the extra $1,000, or whatever the default-insurance cost is, has not been budgeted for – and since it looks like a small amount when weighed against the mortgage itself, it simply gets added on to the loan. A costly oversight.

That's the bad news with default insurance, and about the only good news is that, as with all types of insurance, it can be written off to the extent that it's a legitimate business expense. It means that it's not tax-deductible if the house is used solely as a residence, but that it is partly deductible if the house is being used as an office, or if part of the building is rented out.

Term Life Insurance

Term life insurance is important, but salary continuance is much more so. Most individuals have life insurance at their place of work – a group insurance policy – so for the homeowner with a mortgage, the first thing to weigh up is whether he has enough. It's imperative that he does. Group insurance – generally – is intended to replace your salary for a couple of years – not much more than that – whereas, if you were to die, your mortgage will stay in place until it comes due. And there have been many cases in which a bank would not renew the mortgage of a deceased person because the surviving spouse was not regarded as a good risk.

The second possibility is that there's too much insurance. In the same way that people overinsure their houses, they often over overinsure themselves. Maybe it helps them sleep at night, but if you have a house worth $100,000 do you really NEED a million bucks worth of life insurance? It might be a far better idea to settle for half that amount and use the savings to pay down the mortgage and wipe out a few years of mortgage payments. There are a couple of other options here, too. Decliningvalue insurance, roughly in lockstep with the mortgage and falling in value each year as the loan gets paid off, can make a lot of sense. With a level-term policy, on the other hand, the amount stays the same as the mortgage shrinks. Do you need that extra chunk? That's something you talk about with an insurance agent. But one way or another you must have enough to cover the house itself, the closing off of the mortgage, including discharge penalties and legal fees, plus the other, unforeseen costs that will arise. What this amounts to is a life-insurance policy worth slightly more than the full face value of the loan.

Term life insurance is an extremely competitive area of the insurance market, and such factors as whether a person smokes or not can make a difference in premiums of up to 50 per cent. So it really pays to shop around. And yet some people say to me: "Why bother to insure the mortgage at all? This house is going to appreciate in value, we made a sizable down payment on it, and our equity is increasing all the time. If our chief breadwinner dies, we can always sell if we have to." True enough, they can always sell, but consider: a spouse or family in that situation has already had to experience considerable disruption and grief, and now they have to take over new responsibilities. The bills are not going to be any lower because one less mouth to feed doesn't make a lot of difference, plus there will be the cost of settling up the estate, taking care of unfinished business, and all the rest. Taking all that together, it's an awful lot easier for the family NOT to have to leave the house. Especially if the real estate market happens to have taken a downward lurch. With life insurance in place to cover the mortgage, the survivors of the deceased can ride out the depressed prices, and then, if they do want to sell, do it at the right time.

The person who borrows against a house for the

purpose of investing should try to get the banker to insist on there being life insurance. Why? Because if he does, this now becomes a tax-deductible business cost, no different from the interest on the loan, the lawyer's fees, and all the other expenses relating to the transaction. Needless to say, this does have to be a condition imposed by the bank; a borrower can't "insist" that he insure himself, any more than he can create phony expenses, or pad any of the bills. This is something that often gets missed, and one reason it does is that if you borrow funds, the payments servicing the loan will probably be paid monthly, whereas insurance is most commonly paid with a single annual cheque. It's easy to forget to tie them together.

Interest-Rate Insurance

This is a scheme currently being offered by CMHC as a means of giving the borrower a degree of protection against sudden, sharp increases in interest rates. It was instituted in March 1984 in response to the sky-high rates of the preceding period. Despite its worthy intentions, rates are relatively stable now, so CMHC is getting few takers. With good reason.

Here's how it works. For a 1-1/2-per-cent fee, CMHC will cover the holder of a mortgage for 75 per cent of any increase over and above 2 percentage points, when the mortgage comes due. The guarantee on the new mortgage will be for the same period of time as its predecessor, i.e., if the original was for 5 years, CMHC will offer its protection for 5 years the next time round. A maximum of $70,000 is covered, and the original loan has to have been at market rates, so it's no good getting a bargain-rate mortgage from the vendor, for example, and trying to use that as the base because CMHC won't bite.

Say you take out a $70,000 mortgage at 11 per cent in January 1988. The fee will be $1,050. Renewal time rolls around, in January 1993, and now the going rate is 14 per cent. In this case, CMHC will pick up three-quarters of 1 per cent – the first 2 percentage points representing the "deductible."

Clearly, when rates are falling, the plan is a dead duck – why pay that $1,050 premium if you're never going to collect? If rates start heading up again sharply, it could be a different story, but it's my opinion they won't be allowed to – at least not to the point where paying this insurance would be justified. There are two other things wrong with the scheme. One, $70,000 doesn't always go too far in buying a house in some parts of Canada, and two, the cost of the insurance premium is a fixed 1 1/2 per cent regardless of how long the original mortgage is for; instead of being prorated, the $70,000 worth of coverage will entail the same $1,050 whether the loan is for 6 months, a year, or 5 years.

Property Taxes

It frequently happens that the payment of property taxes is made through the lender, whereby one-twelfth – or, often, more than one-twelfth – of the annual taxes is automatically tacked on to the monthly mortgage payment. The bigger the mortgage, the more likely it is this will happen because to the lender the high-ratio mortgage

is a risk and, in the event of financial problems and unpaid taxes, the municipality gets first crack at the house.
The lender is therefore protecting himself – or so the
theory goes – because the last thing he wants is to have to
go down to City Hall to negotiate to get his house back.
As well, the bank frequently adds on a few bucks every
month in anticipation of tax increases.

For the borrower, this way of doing things is something
to be avoided, if at all possible, because what it means is
that he is paying taxes too rapidly. By leaving the money
in the bank and paying taxes directly every quarter, he'd
be earning interest on that cash. Instead, he's shelling out
once a month and letting the bank make use of the money.
Sometimes this can't be avoided, particularly if the down
payment has been small, but after a period of time, when
part of the mortgage has been paid down, it's worth trying
to negotiate to change the arrangement. Try every year.
And there's another really good reason to pay your own
property taxes. If they suddenly take a jump and the
homeowner is caught short, he's a lot better off owing
money to the municipality than to the bank. Why?
Because the bank will cheerfully add the shortfall to the
principal on the mortgage, meaning it will carry interest
charges for the next 20 years, or whatever period of time is
outstanding on the loan. That's right. Yet more amortization. A $200 shortfall, amortized at 12 per cent over 20
years, will add up to more than $520 by the time it's paid
off – more than 2 1/2 times the original cost. At the same
time, however, remember that the city will also charge interest on the arrears and the net cost will very likely be
higher to the homeowner than if he had taken out a loan
to pay his taxes. So unless he has totally exhausted his borrowing power, owing money to either the bank or the
municipality for back taxes makes no sense. As well,

unpaid taxes can become a headache if the person wants to sell his property. Mind you, the chances are that someone in that situation is probably awful at paying his bills, and, in fact, he's probably the only one who SHOULD let the lender pay his taxes every month because the cost of going into arrears is going to be a lot higher than that of having the money attached to a monthly mortgage payment.

When you get your property-tax assessment, examine it with a fine tooth comb. If there's a major change, be prepared to go back and argue. Property taxes, of course, are calculated through multiplying the assessment by the going mill rate, and both tend to go up all the time; but an assessment can be as wrong as any other estimate. If you feel it's really out of line, one way to contest it is by comparing it with that of your neighbor. But in general there's not much to be done. One extra thought here. If you make changes to a property and apply for a building permit, you can reasonably expect that the house will be reassessed, so don't get one if you don't need to, i.e., if the alterations are minor, or pertaining more to maintenance than renovation. I've heard the term "delayed maintenance" used convincingly. The thinking here is, "I should have done this 10 years ago," and if so, you can make the case that the house has been maintained rather than altered. Now, if you add a room onto the house, don't try to claim that as "late maintenance," but if you repair something that's been steadily deteriorating during those 10 years, that's not unreasonable.

And finally, don't forget once again that if you're renting out part of your house or running a business from it, a portion of your property taxes becomes tax-deductible against your income. Other than that, of course, they're not.

Chapter 12

Magic in Amortization

When interest rates are high, the amortization process is a killer because only tiny, tiny amounts of the monthly payment are going against the principal. And as we've seen, the person who's locked into a variable-rate mortgage, which rises and falls with the bank rate, can actually owe more at the end of the term than he borrowed in the first place, if rates move up sharply and stay there; conversely, the lower the rate, the more damage is being done to the principal each month. With a fixed-rate mortgage, there isn't any of that uncertainty. Nonetheless, an amortization schedule is essential; for a few dollars, a chart can be run off quickly – by a real estate agent, through the bank, by a friend with the right computer program – and it's my opinion that a borrower should no more be without one than without the deed to his house. Only by looking at the figures is it possible to see the mileage you can get from paying extra money – even very small amounts – against the principal on the loan. The savings can be startling.

Let's start by examining a relatively modest $40,000 mortgage. Remember that in all our examples we're just talking about the mortgage itself, not the payment of property taxes, which lending institutions often insist on taking care of, tacking them on to the loan payment. In this case, we have a $40,000 loan with an interest rate of 10 1/2 per cent, amortized over 25 years, and requiring a monthly "blended" payment of $371.34, principal and interest. When the borrower makes his first payment, $28.76 will go toward the principal, while the balance will be interest; the following month, writing an identical cheque, but on a loan that is now a fraction smaller, $29.01 goes against the principal. And so it advances, chipping away at the principal, month after month, year after year – assuming that the interest rate stays constant – until there's a tilt, and the bulk of the payment is going toward principal. In this instance, that point is reached in the 16th year, with payment number 220, when a breakdown of our $371.34 cheque shows that $186.16 is going toward principal and $185.18 on interest. With the last payment of all, number 300, the payment is a shade lower – $360.36 – reflecting the fact that for the final month, the outstanding balance on the loan has fallen to less than a normal monthly payment. On this somewhat momentous occasion, the breakdown consists of $357.30 going toward principal and an almost-invisible $3.06 in interest.

You heave a sigh of relief and burn the mortgage papers. Great going, but, in fact, they could have been burned years before. If the borrower had put even minuscule amounts of extra money against the principal, they would have been. And the key thing to realize in all this is that the earlier on in the mortgage prepayments are made, the greater the savings will be. A single extra monthly payment at the end of the first year of the mortgage wipes out 24 years worth of interest on that amount. The payment is "blended," but nonetheless that's still $371.34 that HASN'T been borrowed for all those years. This is why a mortgage is so deadly if you do things the way the lender would like. On our $40,000 loan, plodding along year after year, the borrower is normally going to put out $71,000 and change in interest charges by the time he's done – almost twice the size of the original loan – producing a total of $111,391.02. And the example we're using here carries a relatively low interest rate.

What the borrower should do is set up certain financial parameters, so he can say, "What are the merits of doing A, as opposed to B?" If we take the $40,000 mortgage and decide – arbitrarily – to add $20 a month to the payment, then that will cost us an extra buck for each working day. That's not exactly a fortune – the change in a person's pocket would carry it most of the time – but see what happens by nudging up the monthly payment to $391.34 and holding it there for the lifetime of the mortgage. The original total will plummet to $95,571.57 and the length of the mortgage term will fall to 20 years, 5 months. That dollar a day – less than half a pack of cigarettes, a couple of cups of coffee, half the price of a beer in a restaurant – will have obliterated 4 1/2 years worth of payments, which in cash translates into $15,819.45.

And if you think that's a big saving, look at what happens if you – just once a year – arbitrarily pay an extra $500 against the principal: perhaps when you get your income-tax refund, or a bonus at work, or decide to cash in a Canada Savings Bond, whatever. The net saving through that one-shot deal every year will be an astonishing $24,414.59, cutting the life of the loan to 17 years, 8 months. And this can be done through something as simple as buying a Canada Savings Bond at work once a year, through the payroll-deduction system. If there are two earners in a household and they were each to buy a bond in that way and each slap the $500 against the mortgage every year, then those $1,000 increments would wipe out 11 years on a 25-year mortgage, for a net saving of about $35,000. Eleven years! In this case, almost half the interest on the loan has now disappeared, so we're talking about a major, major saving, at a cost of less than $20 a week: our dollar a day plus perhaps a visit to the movies.

One detail to note is that whatever the nature of the loan, prepaying by means of a round sum will necessitate having a fresh amortization table calculated each time, which you won't have to do if you prepay in multiples of your normal monthly payment. As long as you're prepared to "round up," rather than "round down," then most of the time you can disregard the $10 or $12 cost of getting a new schedule run off; it's insignificant when weighed against the benefit of having even a couple of dollars go to work for the years remaining on the mortgage.

These days, most of the large lending institutions allow a borrower to prepay up to 10 per cent of a mortgage annually, and in this case that would be $4,000. If that $4,000 extra was paid each year, we'd save more than $54,000 and slash the mortgage to 7 years, 1 month which is as close to beating the pants off the bank as a person is ever likely to get. But needless to say, the chances are that our borrower doesn't have a lump sum of $4,000. Or perhaps he does, but not at the right time; some mortgages only allow prepayments to be made on the anniversary

date, which might be exactly the point at which the borrower is short of cash. In that situation, one course that's
open, and which is extremely viable, is to borrow the
money.

Borrowing more money to pay off part of an existing
debt sounds like something Al Capone would encourage
you to do, but the fact is it's often a very good idea. If our
homeowner were to borrow that $4,000 with a conven-
tional short-term loan at 12 per cent, and apply it to the
mortgage, he's going to end up way ahead. And provided
his credit rating is good, there's no reason why he
shouldn't get the money from the same lender who holds
that mortgage: the lender not only still has the house as
collateral, he can also see that its original loan is actually
going to be more secure than ever. Here's why.

If the homeowner were to borrow that $4,000 at 12 per
cent every year for 6 years, and use the money to pay
down the principal on the mortgage, then he'd be able to
burn the mortgage papers in 7 years. The 1-year loan will
call for a monthly payment of $354.86 – producing a total
of $4,258.32. (Notice here, incidentally, that in the same
way as with any other amortization schedule, the total interest on the short-term loan is actually less than 12 per
cent of $4,000 (which is $480) because the payments are
knocking down the principal each month.) So every year
he borrows; and every year he pays down the big mortgage. After 6 years, these short-term loans have added up
to $25,549.92 – and in the meantime reduced the total
cost of the mortgage to $52,641. So there's a net saving of
more than $27,000, plus the thing is paid off in 7 years, 6
months. And that's only 5 months longer than if the person had not had to borrow the $4,000 each year, but hap-
pened to have the cash.

But let's assume that the borrower is really strapped for

cash and the absolute maximum extra he could afford to pay on the $40,000 is one additional payment a year (such as in the case we described in the chapter on weekly mortgages). If you cast an eye over to Table A showing how our $40,000, 10-1/2-per-cent loan progresses over its long, miserable 25-year life, then you'll see that after the 12th payment, at the end of year 1, the balance outstanding is $39,638.16. If a 13th payment of $371.34 were to be made at that point, the balance would immediately dip to $39,266.82. Okay, now trace the "balance of loan" column of figures downward and the closest figure to our new total of $39,266.82 is $39,272.32, and that's what would have been owed after payment number 23, in the original scheme of things. It would have taken 11 more payments to have reached that point, instead of which they've been wiped off the ledger forever by making one additional payment; a total of $4,084.74 has been saved through paying $371.34, a net gain of $3,713.4, in tax-free dollars.

So when we say there's magic in all this, we mean it. A lot of people probably wish they had a $40,000 mortgage a 10 1/2 per cent, but regardless of the three variables that remain in there – the amount borrowed, the interest rate, and the amortization period – the calculation holds true. And clearly, the larger all those factors are – in particular the second two – then the more advantage there is to this kind of footwork.

Proof? Let's now look at a bigger mortgage (Table B) with a higher interest rate: $65,000, amortized over 25 years at 11 1/2 per cent and requiring a monthly payment of $648.09. If the borrower pays it off over the quarter-century laid down in the agreement, then at the end of it all he'll have paid back the $65,000 plus $129,426.03 in interest: a total cost of $194,426.03. Instead, he too decides to put an extra $20 a month toward the principal – the

SAMPLE AMORTIZATION TABLE A

AMOUNT: 40000.000 BLENDED.   PAYMENTS: $371.34
PAYABLE: MONTHLY   PRINT: TO MATURITY
RATE %: 10.5000   COMPOUNDED: SEMIANNUAL.
EFFECTIVE RATE %: .0085645152
STARTING DATE: MAY 1, 1978
FIRST PAYMENT DUE: JUNE 1, 1978

Payment Number	Payment Date	Total Payment	Interest Payment	Principal Payment	Balance of Loan
1	JUNE 1, 1978	371.34	342.58	28.76	39971.24
2	JULY 1, 1978	371.34	342.33	29.01	39942.23
3	AUG 1, 1978	371.34	342.09	29.25	39912.98
4	SEPT 1, 1978	371.34	341.84	29.50	39883.48
5	OCT 1, 1978	371.34	341.58	29.76	39853.72
6	NOV 1, 1978	371.34	341.33	30.01	39823.71
7	DEC 1, 1978	371.34	341.07	30.27	39793.44
8	JAN 1, 1979	371.34	340.81	30.53	39762.91
9	FEB 1, 1979	371.34	340.55	30.79	39732.12
10	MAR 1, 1979	371.34	340.29	31.05	39701.07
11	APR 1, 1979	371.34	340.02	31.32	39669.75
12	MAY 1, 1979	371.34	339.75	31.59	39638.16
13	JUNE 1, 1979	371.34	339.48	31.86	39606.30
14	JULY 1, 1979	371.34	339.21	32.13	39574.17
15	AUG 1, 1979	371.34	338.93	32.41	39541.76
16	SEPT 1, 1979	371.34	338.66	32.68	39509.08
17	OCT 1, 1979	371.34	338.38	32.96	39476.12
18	NOV 1, 1979	371.34	338.09	33.25	39442.87
19	DEC 1, 1979	371.34	337.81	33.53	39409.34
20	JAN 1, 1980	371.34	337.52	33.82	39375.52
21	FEB 1, 1980	371.34	337.23	34.11	39341.41
22	MAR 1, 1980	371.34	336.94	34.40	39307.01
23	APR 1, 1980	371.34	336.65	34.69	39272.32
24	MAY 1, 1980	371.34	336.35	34.99	39237.33
25	JUNE 1, 1980	371.34	336.05	35.29	39202.04
26	JULY 1, 1980	371.34	335.75	35.59	39166.45
27	AUG 1, 1980	371.34	335.44	35.90	39130.55
28	SEPT 1, 1980	371.34	335.13	36.21	39094.34
29	OCT 1, 1980	371.34	334.82	36.52	39057.82
30	NOV 1, 1980	371.34	334.51	36.83	39020.99

SAMPLE AMORTIZATION TABLE B

AMOUNT: 65000.000 BLENDED.   PAYMENTS: $648.09
PAYABLE: MONTHLY   PRINT: TO MATURITY
RATE %: 11.5000   COMPOUNDED: SEMIANNUAL.
EFFECTIVE RATE %: .0093614858
STARTING DATE: DEC 1, 1978
FIRST PAYMENT DUE: JAN 1, 1979

Payment Number	Payment Date	Total Payment	Interest Payment	Principal Payment	Balance of Loan
1	JAN 1, 1979	648.09	608.50	39.59	64960.41
2	FEB 1, 1979	648.09	608.13	39.96	64920.45
3	MAR 1, 1979	648.09	607.75	40.34	64880.11
4	APR 1, 1979	648.09	607.37	40.72	64839.39
5	MAY 1, 1979	648.09	606.99	41.10	64798.29
6	JUNE 1, 1979	648.09	606.61	41.48	64756.81
7	JULY 1, 1979	648.09	606.22	41.87	64714.94
8	AUG 1, 1979	648.09	605.83	42.26	64672.68
9	SEPT 1, 1979	648.09	605.43	42.66	64630.02
10	OCT 1, 1979	648.09	605.03	43.06	64586.96
11	NOV 1, 1979	648.09	604.63	43.46	64543.50
12	DEC 1, 1979	648.09	604.22	43.87	64499.63
13	JAN 1, 1980	648.09	603.81	44.28	64455.35
14	FEB 1, 1980	648.09	603.40	44.69	64410.66
15	MAR 1, 1980	648.09	602.98	45.11	64365.55
16	APR 1, 1980	648.09	602.56	45.53	64320.02
17	MAY 1, 1980	648.09	602.13	45.96	64274.06
18	JUNE 1, 1980	648.09	601.70	46.39	64227.67
19	JULY 1, 1980	648.09	601.27	46.82	64180.85
20	AUG 1, 1980	648.09	600.83	47.26	64133.59
21	SEPT 1, 1980	648.09	600.39	47.70	64085.89
22	OCT 1, 1980	648.09	599.94	48.15	64037.74
23	NOV 1, 1980	648.09	599.49	48.60	63989.14
24	DEC 1, 1980	648.09	599.03	49.06	63948.08
25	JAN 1, 1981	648.09	598.57	49.52	63890.56
26	FEB 1, 1981	648.09	598.11	49.98	63840.58
27	MAR 1, 1981	648.09	597.64	50.45	63790.13
28	APR 1, 1981	648.09	597.17	50.92	63739.21
29	MAY 1, 1981	648.09	596.69	51.40	63687.81
30	JUNE 1, 1981	648.09	596.21	51.88	63635.93

same dollar for every business day – creating a monthly payment of $668.09. That dollar a day will save him $20,933.30 in interest charges, and trim the life of the mortgage to 21 years and 7 months. Were he, however, to arbitrarily decide he could put an extra $600 a year toward the mortgage principal, he'd end up saving himself $38,402 and cut the mortgage to 18 years, 2 months, while an extra $1,000 annually would save him almost $52,000 and give him a 16-year mortgage.

On the other hand, perhaps a single extra payment of $648.09 is the absolute ceiling our borrower can afford. Look at the loan chart in this case and, again, go to payment number 12, after which he owes $64,499.63. By making a dent in the principal to the tune of another $648.09, the sum is reduced to $63,851.54. In the case of the $40,000 mortgage at 10 1/2 per cent, we saw that the borrower had saved himself 10 payments by making an extra one. But with a higher mortgage at a higher rate, the saving is more: the new, reduced principal in this case would not have been reached until after the 25th payment – 13 payments, or $8,425.17 later. So make that 13th payment now, at the end of the first year, and there's a net saving of $7,777.08. In fact, the real saving will be greater than that because the new, lower total amount owing on the principal would normally have been reached at a point closer to the 26th payment than to the 25th. And, as we also discussed in the chapter on weekly mortgages, the time to do this – if possible – is not at the end of the year, but at the beginning, which will put that extra money to work for a whole additional year.

Whenever we do it, what's really amazing – and very easy to overlook – is the fact that those savings are tax-free. The average person's mortgage is not tax-deductible – although, as we know by now, it can be made so – and where it is not, then $9,000 worth of mortgage payments represents a great deal more than that: in the 40-per-cent tax bracket that person has to earn $15,000 before he takes home $9,000. In effect, saving money on mortgage payments allows the borrower to avoid having to produce income that would otherwise be taxed.

Despite the powerful logic of paying down a mortgage, the fact is that a person who's making payments every month will often balk at shelling out still more when a bit of extra cash comes around; there's got to be more to life than loan payments, he thinks defensively, and promptly spends that windfall, or goes on a holiday. As we've seen, the lower the interest rate on the mortgage, the less dramatic are the results of this forced-savings strategy. In our first situation, the borrower might say, "The loan's at 10 1/2 per cent, that's not so bad." Up to a point he's right, but boy, when the meter's ticking on a 16-per-cent loan, the inducement to do something about it gets pretty persuasive. Or even at 12 per cent.

The real trick lies in deciding how much you can afford to pay because, remember, the loan charts and schedules that the lender pulls out of his drawer are guides, no more than that. If a person adds up all his expenses and decides he can afford monthly payments of exactly $800 a month, then that's the figure he should go by. Provided he's within the bank's minimum-income criteria and isn't over-extending himself, he shouldn't have any trouble getting a "custom" loan. Another detail is that by going with a rounded-off figure, the progress of the loan is easier to monitor and there's less scope for error. In this instance, that $800 a month could obtain a $74,000 mortgage for the borrower, at 12 per cent, which is about as typical a situation as I can think of. Amortized over 20 years, it calls for a monthly payment of $799.93. Say by the end of the first year he's accumulated a modest $400 – half a normal payment – that he can pay against the principal, which stands at $73,013.99. Even by shaving the balance down to just $72,613.99, he's still saved himself four payments, less the $400. He's effectively made a profit of $2,800, tax-free, with an investment one-seventh that amount. Can you tell me of any other investment where you can guarantee a return like that? If he puts a full payment against the principal, it becomes almost an eightfold return, and so it progresses.

Because, in all these cases, it's the interest on the loan that the borrower is escaping. It follows that the further he progresses down the amortization schedule, the more the payments will flatten out, and the less dramatic the savings will be. As we've said, the "tilt" in the composition of the monthly payment – the stage at which more money is going on principal than on interest – occurs somewhere during the second half of the loan. Because an amortization schedule contains a breakdown of each individual monthly payment, that point of arrival can be seen at a glance. It's important to know exactly where it does occur, but even in the last years of the mortgage, the theory still holds. Going back to our first example, the $40,000 loan at 10 1/2 per cent, and assuming that there have been no prepayments during all those years (not a heartening thought), then at the beginning of the final year, number 25, there will be a balance of $4,207.70 outstanding. Making an extra payment of $371.34, the normal monthly amount, the borrower will lower the balance to $3,836.36 and end up making his final payment one month earlier than he would otherwise have done.

We've said that a bank will – perhaps with a bit of prodding – grant a "custom" loan. That's generally true, but at the same time, however, it's unlikely to offer one, and this raises a point in the case of borrowers whose original mortgage was at, or near, the limit of what the institution would lend. What can happen here is that the mortgage comes due, and the bank suggests to the borrower that he now renew it on terms that would keep to the mortgage schedule by maintaining payments at around the existing level, or even by lowering them. This time around, those payments might be significantly LESS than the borrower could afford a) because some of the principal has been paid down and b) because he now has more money coming in. For a second the offer looks attractive, but, in fact, with his improved circumstances, the old payment schedule is exactly what the borrower doesn't want because, as always, he should be paying as much as he can afford.

Equally, if renewal time rolls around and interest rates have fallen, the institution may well offer to renew at the existing rate of payment, or a lower one. If the borrower is unwise enough to accept, because he likes the look of the new, lower payment being offered, he's needlessly locking himself into extra years of amortization. If you were able to afford $800 a month at 12 per cent, and you can get a new mortgage at 9 per cent, then at the VERY LEAST you should keep on paying the $800, preferably more than that, because the lower the rate, the more of the principal gets paid off each month. In the case of a $50,000 loan, amortized over 25 years at 10 per cent, $489.57 of the principal would have been paid off at the end of the first year. At 12 per cent – even though the monthly payment has been larger ($447.25 and $515.95 respectively) – the balance will have fallen by only $417.26; while with a 14-per-cent loan, which will need a cheque of $586.94 to service it every month, only $254.62 of the original $50,000 will have been paid off. A mortgage is the last thing in the world that should lure a person into "saving" a few dollars each month through lowered payments because the name of the game is beating the amortization schedule – not getting sucked into it – and the only way to do that is to pay off as much of the loan as you can, in the shortest time possible.

For exactly that reason, another serious mistake at renewal time is to reamortize over the same period of time as the first time around, i.e., to pay off a 25-year mortgage for, say, 3 years, and then refinance on the basis of another 25 years. Similarly, misguided people anxious to raise cash without increasing their monthly payments sometimes refinance through stretching out the amortization on a mortgage. This is a mug's game. That person would be far, far better off getting almost any kind of consumer loan, even over a period of 5 years, than in trapping themselves in that relentless compounding of interest that takes place when money is amortized over 20 or 30 years.

That's why, if he can, a borrower should seek not just to pay down his mortgage, but to start out with as short-term an amortization period as possible because, here too, the savings are enormous. If we take the case of a $50,000 mortgage, amortized over 25 years at 11 per cent, the monthly payment will be $481.27, whereas over 24 years, it's $485.32. A full year of payments – $5,775 – can be wiped out by paying the extra 4 bucks a month – $1,152 over the 24 years – and the result is a net saving of $4,623. And in exactly the same way, see what happens to the person who foolishly goes for a mortgage of 35 years – and some institutions will certainly lend on those terms. That same $50,000 mortgage is now serviced with a monthly cheque of $458.99 – a difference of $22.28 per month as compared with the payments on the 25-year term. Let's hope he enjoys that $22 a month because he's got an extra 10 years of making payments to do so. If the borrower is still alive at the end of all this, he might sit down and see that the $22.28, over the first 25 years of the loan, apparently saved him $6,684. Over the final 10 years, of course, he didn't save anything in loan payments because there wouldn't have been any. And then comes the moment of truth: over the 35 years, he will have parted with a total of $192,775.08. Take away his $22.28 monthly "saving" and the final figure is $186,009.18, whereas the man with the 25-year mortgage paid back, in all, $144,381 – a difference of $41,628.18. To stretch out that already-huge debt for an additional 10 years has cost the borrower almost as much again as the original loan. So when we use the word "deadly," in talking about amortization, we do so advisedly.

If we stay with our $50,000 loan and reduce the amortization to 20 years, that requires a monthly payment cheque of $507.82, as compared to $481.27 over a 25-year period. The difference is $26.55, but that difference – less than a dollar a day in every calendar month – knocks 5 whole years of mortgage payments off the loan, with a net saving of just over $22,500. If you go down to 15 years, the monthly payment is $560.67. The difference between that and the payment for the 25-year term is just under 80 bucks, which looks like a lot until you add up the net saving. In this case, the total amount of money that the borrower has parted with is $100,920.60 – a $43,460.40 saving over the 25-year term. Many borrowers go for 10-year mortgages, and they're smart to do so. In this instance, with a monthly payment of $681.87 – $200 more than with the 25-year amortization – the total cost of the mortgage will be $81,824.40 and the net saving an amazing $67,386.34. Fifteen whole years of mortgage payments have been obliterated by paying an extra amount of less than $50 a week.

This is really the way to pick a mortgage – by juggling with the amortization period. You find the best possible interest rate, decide on the maximum you can afford – and we do mean that, because if you overextend yourself you're going to hate your new house – and then follow the chart through the "years" column to the point where the two figures meet. If it's at 13 years, then forget about 10 years or 15 years – get a 13-year mortgage. If the property is expensive and it takes every nickel you have to get into it, then you may well have to go with a 25-year term, and providing you're happy with the investment, then fine. But where buyers often go wrong is in opting needlessly for the 25-year mortgage because it's "cheaper." They couldn't be more wrong.

You see, it's not just the day-to-day savings that we're seeing here, in playing with amortization; it's also the fact that the house is almost certainly rising in value at the same time. Sure, prices can go up and down in the short term. But between 1976 and 1989, the average price of a house in Canada went up from $61,389 to $264,257. When it's time to look back at the 1990s, we'll probably see a still more pronounced increase. Getting a firm hand on amortization and making it go to work for you, rather than the other way round, is the best way to do even better. Where can you go into a store and buy something that's rising in value and which is on sale? And never lose sight of the fact that if you can shorten the life of your mortgage and save $1,000, then that's $1,000 that you didn't have to earn. A person who loses one-third of their paycheque to the tax-man each week has had to earn $1,500 to bring home that $1,000. And finally, don't forget that paying down the principal on the loan is the best possible insurance against the possibility that when it's renewal time, interest rates will have gone up.

People sometimes say to me: "I don't want to pay off my mortgage early because when the time comes to sell, an existing mortgage with an attractive interest rate gives the buyer an extra option." On occasion that's true, such as in the case of a buyer who's at the outer limits of his financing, but usually it isn't true. If you buy a house for $50,000 and sell it for $100,000, the buyer probably doesn't want anything to do with your existing $25,000 mortgage, even though it may be at a low rate. Why? Because if he takes it over, the very next thing he has to do is secure secondary financing for the balance, and the interest rate on that second mortgage will likely be several points higher than on the first. Automatically. For that reason, a "no mortgage" situation, in which the buyer is free to arrange all his own financing, gives the most flexibility. Who wants a second mortgage? You're usually far better off with a single high-ratio loan, even though it may have to be insured.

So you always – ALWAYS – pay down the mortgage, wherever and whenver you can. But at the same time, if rates are low and a seller thinks they're going to take a hike, there's no reason why he shouldn't refinance to take advantage of the current situation. Of course, there are situations in which people do this even when the house has been completely paid off. Then if rates do jump, the existing mortgage can – and I say "can" – look good to a buyer, depending on a) the rates at the time, b) the buyer's circumstances, and c) the percentage of the house price that the existing mortgage represents. This last factor is important because it's one thing to assume a mortgage that covers 60 or 70 per cent of the house price and quite another to take over a 20-per-cent mortgage that will now significantly jack up the price of the second. By and large, the buyer is better off with either no mortgage at all or else with a big one that covers most of the financing. What he doesn't want is to have to inherit a dinky little first mortgage.

Another objection to prepaying mortgages is that, as an investment, it's too fixed: equity in a house doesn't have the same liquidity as money in the bank. With a high-ratio mortgage that may be true, but I say that for most people the merit of this flexibility pales when set against escaping – even by a tiny amount – the burden of paying interest on interest, for years or decades at a time. I also hear it said that since the purchasing power of the dollar constantly shrinks, then borrowed money is worth more than money that's paid back – so don't pay back more than you have to. That's nonsense, as well. We started out by looking at a $40,000 mortgage and discovered we could save a total of $15,819.45 over its 25-year life by the simple expedient of paying an extra dollar for each working day – $20 a month. There's simply no way those savings could be equaled, or even approached, by holding on to that dollar a day.

Refinancing a mortgage so as to provide a selling tool, or any other ploy, is therefore the kind of move that should be made in conjunction with paying down the principal on the loan, not as a substitute for it. And at no time do those prepayments make a greater difference than in the early years. The word "mortgage" is French in origin and literally means "dead pledge" – i.e., it expires when the last payment has been made. A borrower might be forgiven for thinking the translation should be: "Pledged until I'm dead," because what makes the mortgage such a burden is the ceaseless compounding of interest on interest, and if you let the loan run its natural course, it's a real killer.

But by turning things around and declaring war,

through a system of prepayments, what is happening in effect is that it's now the borrower's savings that are getting compounded, year after year. And therein lies the magic.

Chapter 13

Interest Rates: Up or Down?

If everybody with a mortgage was given a crystal ball and was allowed one question, this is the one they'd probably ask. In days gone by, certainly from the 1950s to the 1970s, interest rates didn't matter a whole lot because they hardly varied. That sense of security disappeared along with the 25-year mortgage. Then, as we all know, interest rates took off, culminating in the 20-per-cent levels that made borrowing such a dicey proposition in the first 2 years of the 1980s. Personally, I don't think we'll see a repeat of that cycle; there are too many reasons why not. At the same time, we have to recognize that what that upward surge did was forever change the banking rules.

And not necessarily for the worse, because, in fact, it's the very volatility of the mortgage game, these days, that makes it playable. Some win, some take a bath. A 6-month bargain-basement mortgage – in the early months of 1987, some of the major institutions were offering

6-month mortgages at 8 per cent – can obviously save a homeowner a substantial amount of money: a $100,000 mortgage at that level calls for a monthly payment of $763.22, whereas a 10-per-cent mortgage costs $894.49, and, as we've noted, the lower the interest rate, the more of the principal is being paid down every month. At the same time, however, a buyer whose resources are already stretched and who opts for the cheapest possible mortgage – a short-term one – may be sowing the seeds of financial disaster in the event that rates subsequently move sharply. Now, if that person's a real gambler, he might then decide to stick with short-term, low-cost mortgages, and find himself visiting the bank every 6 months to renegotiate. That's fine, as long as he doesn't mind living that way, but most people need a bit more security than that. In the end, he would do better to compromise and settle for a medium-term mortgage at a middling rate that will, if nothing else, provide a sufficient cushion in the event of a loss of earning power, or other setback. Three-year mortgages remain the most common, and no doubt there are a number of recent buyers in Southern Ontario who by now have realized why, having leaped into an overheated market with both feet and opted for the cheapest mortgage they could get. If a person has a $150,000 mortgage on a house, then a 1-percentage-point hike in rates, going from our 8-per-cent rate to 9 (which is still a pretty modest increase) will change his monthly payment by almost $100 – from $1,144.84 to $1,241.98. With a 2-percentage-point increase, it's almost a $200 monthly increase – $2,400 a year, which for a person in the 40-per-cent tax bracket, with a non-tax-deductible mortgage, translates into another $3,600 that has to be earned. And as we know all too well, there's nothing unusual in the least about a 2-point increase. All of which means that as the rates move up and down, they provide a constant opportunity to play the market, and some people can afford to gamble more than others.

The 3-year mortgage is thus a good bet for the individual whose resources are stretched. But at the same time, in a period of interest-rate stability – and I think that's what we're looking at, for the next few years – my strong feeling is that the way to really come out ahead is to go for a low-cost, 6-month mortgage – and pay an artificially inflated monthly payment. Ask the lender for a 6-month mortgage and tell him you'll pay the 5-year rate. So now your monthly payment is $100 or $200 more than it needs to be, and, as we've shown, doing things that way will save you substantial sums of money. And the lender won't have any trouble with that arrangement, either. It may be argued that there's the constantly recurring cost of arranging a new mortgage every month, but the fees are going to be comparatively small when weighed against 1) the cost of the mortgage itself, which is going to be rock-bottom, 2) the fact that with the low-cost loan more of the principal is being paid down every month, and 3) the fact that you have much greater access to the mortgage, because it opens up every 6 months. This means that not only can lump sums be paid against the principal at those intervals but also, if interest rates change sharply, or if you reap a windfall of some type, you can get out at relatively short notice.

But with that said, how do you know which way – and, more important, when – to jump? You do so by picking the brains of anybody who makes it their business to have a handle on these things – your banker, your accountant, your stockbroker, your lawyer, your insurance agent, real estate agents – and they'll all have an opinion. But what are the factors they use to base it on?

I, myself, first and foremost watch the world markets, and in particular I'm interested in the state of the dollar – the Canadian dollar, whose fortunes rise and fall with its U.S. counterpart. If a currency comes under pressure vis à vis the other main ones, a good way to support it, unsurprisingly, is for the central bank – the Bank of Canada, and the Federal Reserve – to increase short-term interest rates. Why? Because that's where foreign investors deal – 24 hours a day, by means of electronic fund transfers – and investors are constantly on the move, from market to market and from country to country, where stocks are often interlisted. This wheeling and dealing in currencies all happens incredibly fast, and often deceptively so, obscuring the fact that the factors that really count, in tilting interest-rate trends upward or downward, move in much, much large cycles, often of about 4 years. Don't get either alarmed or elated at short-term changes.

Needless to say, whatever happens south of the border will be felt here, too, and the number-one force at work on the U.S. dollar is the state of the U.S. economy. The better it's doing, the more foreign Japanese yen, West German marks, British pounds, and French francs will want to come in. Conversely, if the economy is performing poorly, that capital will want to leave, and Washington won't be able to sell its bonds, Treasury bills, and other short-term investments – unless interest rates are prodded upward.

But the biggest impact on rates, by far, is made by inflation. If inflation rises, logic tells you that interest rates will too, because investors will be demanding inflation plus something extra – either that or they go elsewhere. And if inflation's running at 4 per cent and the investor's offered only 6 per cent, he may not stick around either because by the time he's paid his tax bill, he may end up in the red.

Interest rates can be, and are, deliberately forced higher as a means of breaking an inflationary trend and that's what was happening in 1980 and 1981. Making money expensive to borrow was a tactic used to slow down consumer spending, not just by Ottawa, but by most of the Western world. And it worked. Meanwhile, those borrowers who reasoned at the time – correctly – that things could only go so far before they turned around, and who therefore took out variable-rate mortgages, came out winners. And again I'll mention my friends who paid off their house in 5 years that way, without once increasing their monthly payment. I do think that the upward spike we saw in the first years of this decade was a once-in-a-lifetime phenomenon. Breaking the inflationary cycle that was being experienced was something that had to be done, and those homeowners who had stretched themselves too far – or, more commonly, had not allowed for the possibility of the layoffs that accompanied the austerity measures – were the Canadians who paid the price.

Something else to consider, in weighing the likely direction of interest rates, is whether there is a significant amount of pent-up demand for housing. If a given market is strong, that may keep rates competitive. Equally, it can make the institutions greedy, and in the rush to borrow, consumers all too often don't take the time and trouble to shop around in the way that they will in a depressed market, when the lending institutions are having trouble putting their money on the street.

A lot of people monitor the weekly change in the Bank of Canada rate – the rate at which it lends money to the individual banks – but it's important to remember this is only a short-term guide, no more than that, which the government uses to show the institutions where it wants interest rates to be. The lower interest rates are, the more likely it is that mortgage rates, particularly short-term ones, will be affected by the weekly rise and fall of the Bank of Canada rate because the banks have less room to maneuver. At the same time, any realistic analysis of interest rates must be based on a curve – a long-term curve that will contain other, short-term cycles. The Bank of Canada might decide, this month, or this year, that in order to support the dollar it has to increase its lending rate. This in turn fuels inflation and recession – which bring rates down again. So it might well be that the curve on a chart will show interest rates to be increasing in the short term, while falling in the long term.

This is by no means unusual, and there is a real danger inherent in thinking that because one interest rate rose, everything else will as well. Back in 1981, someone looking at a graph of rates would have been able to see that the prime rate – the rate offered by institutions to their best corporate customers – was at 22 3/4 per cent, while mortgages were at 18 1/2, i.e., short-term money was more expensive than long-term money. That's not normally how things are – any economist knows that historically it's the other way around, that the cost of a mortgage tends to be HIGHER than that of a loan – so it wasn't that hard to see that things were temporarily out of whack, and were therefore likely to change. Borrowers who realized this and took on variable-rate mortgages had to pluck up some courage, but they sure came out winners at the end.

That's the reason that the 6-month-mortgage game has become so popular: 6 months, short as it is, is nonetheless long enough to permit a look at the bigger picture. The 6-month mortgage, remember, is really more akin to a corporate loan, which fluctuates every day, than to a mortgage, and it has the same attractions and the same potential pitfalls.

And don't forget the deficit. It sometimes happens that a government increases interest rates because it badly needs to obtain some extra cash, and a burgeoning deficit may be the reason why. So when Canada Savings Bonds are being offered with a yield of 19 1/2 per cent, which is a powerful inducement to buy, that in turn will mean that the financial system is obliged to lend out that money again at a higher rate still. And in that way inflation does, literally, spiral upward, as consumers hoard their cash. Likewise, when the economy is really plodding along, any movement toward lower rates pumps up spending because, now, people – or, more to the point, corporations – don't merely spend their savings, they also tend to borrow because the cost of loans is cheap.

All too often, people with a mortgage that's coming due wait until the actual date on which it matures to renew. Instead, they should consider a "preemptive strike." If a 3-year, or say, a 5-year mortgage is due 6 months from now, and the indicators are that rates are going to rise, then you have every reason to move first, and perhaps ask the lender to advance the renewal date – without penalty – on the basis that you're willing to go for another 3- or 5-year term. And if the decision is at the banker's discretion, then he has every reason to at least consider your suggestion because, as a merchant of money, his job is to try to lock you in again, and for as long as possible, rather than see you take that very profitable mortgage to the bank down the street. And, if necessary, you should certainly remind him that renewing the mortgage with a different institution is an option you have available. You may not want to get locked into a long-term loan, so perhaps you can dicker here, and settle on a 2-year term.

Interest rates move up and down and anybody who borrows money should watch them like a hawk and plan accordingly. But don't lose sight of the fact that the quality of the investment is at least as important as the month-to-month cost of financing it. Whatever happens to interest rates, you're better off most of the time owning a piece of property than in renting one and making someone else rich. And once you have some equity, don't sacrifice it without a very good reason – such as investing in another venture that's as good, or better – because in a strong housing market, it's a heck of a lot easier to get out of the market than it is to get back in. Maybe you decide you want to go and live in a cabin for a year to write a book, or to travel the world; it's the same thing: unless there are strong indications the market is going to crash, hold on to the house and rent it out. The rent will stay constant or rise, while the mortgage principal will shrink, even if only marginally, and at the end of it all, you own a piece of property that's increased in value. My parents built a house in Florida, at Port Charlotte. In the first winter, they rented it out and made enough money to pay not only for the upkeep and maintenance, but also for a winter vacation in Spain. Interest rates rise and fall, and they make a powerful difference to a person's financial position. But in the final analysis, they're less important than the overall health of the commodity the money is being used for. You're better off with a high-cost mortgage in a buoyant market than with a 5-per-cent loan in a depressed one.

So there really is money in your mortgage. But what if you don't have a mortgage? More to the point, what if you can't afford one because the price of housing in your city has skyrocketed? As most people know, it's tough to buy a house – or at any rate an affordable house – without a 25-per-cent down payment. That's true, and in the next chapter we'll have a look at some of the basics of current lending policies and practices, as well as at some of the costs that a buyer, especially a first-time buyer, should expect to incur. And we'll see that there can be more here than meets the eye. The reader who has bought a house, or who has sizable assets and can readily put her hands on that 25-per-cent down payment, might want to skim through this next chapter. Because what I'm going to do is to show, using a case history, how it's possible – without going out on a limb and without having to sell the family jewels – to break into a highly priced market.

Chapter 14

Getting a Mortgage

It was just before Christmas of 1986 when John and Judy got the letter from their landlord telling them they had 60 days notice to vacate their comfortable Toronto apartment, their home for the previous 5 years. First they panicked, then they started to think. Circumstances dictated they stay downtown, but beyond that, they decided, everything was negotiable.

Since they knew, somewhat vaguely, that the price of real estate had gone up in the past 2 years – they didn't realize it had gone through the roof – their first instinct was to rent another 2-bedroom apartment. After some inquiries, they discovered that rents had gone haywire, too. Toronto's rent-control laws didn't apply to units renting for more than $750 per month and it was precisely those apartments in the $700-$900 range – which was the amount they decided they could afford – that were in short supply. It looked like they were going to have to spend anything up to $1,000 a month on rent, with no protection against further increases. Because of commitments, their financial circumstances were unlikely to change for another 3 years, and they didn't need a calculator to compute that at the end of that time they'd have spent a minimum of $36,000 and have absolutely nothing to show for it. Worse, as various real estate agents were quick to point out, if they thought house prices were impossible now, wait until 3 years down the road. "The train," as one agent cheerfully put it, "is leaving the station."

John and Judy didn't have any debts, and so, with about $25,000 saved, a dependable joint annual gross income of about $43,000, plus a good credit rating, they thought they were in reasonably good shape, especially in light of the fact that interest rates were low. When they went to the bank to see what sort of a loan they were good for, they learned that one rule of thumb used by lending institutions is that the total cost of running the house – mortgage payments, property taxes, insurance, utilities – should not exceed one-third of the household's gross income. That, however, means existing income, which is the only set of figures the bank is interested in; the fact that a person may be expecting additional income, for whatever reason, is usually irrelevant. In their case, that one-third worked out to just over $14,000. Scanning a chart of mortgage payments, they saw that if they could qualify for a 4-year 10-per-cent mortgage of $100,000, the loan would require monthly payments of just under $900 a month. Staying within the one-third guidelines, that would leave them with $266 a month for taxes and the other house expenses, which would surely be more than enough.

They spent some time discussing the pros and cons of

taking a chance on a short-term mortgage. The cheapest loan in sight, for that same $100,000, was at 8 1/2 per cent, for 6 months, requiring a monthly payment of $795.37. A 1-year mortgage at 9 per cent, from the same institution, would cost $827.98 per month, while the price tag on a 2-year mortgage at 9 1/4 per cent would be $844.45. John and Judy knew people who were gambling with 6-month mortgages, and there were others who had opted for floating, variable-rate loans, which were open. In the latter case, the borrowers were calculating that the smartest thing to do was to float with the bank rate, which was in any case low, until it showed signs of moving upward, and then to lock into a fixed-rate mortgage. You pay more for an open mortgage, of course, and it was arguable whether those borrowers ended up ahead because bank rates only moved up marginally in the next few months.

The real question that has to be asked is whether the borrower can afford to gamble. If he is able to absorb the punishment of a sharp rise in rates, then well and good, but John and Judy decided that since their resources would be stretched, then in light of the fact that their financial situation was unlikely to change for 3 years or so, they should play it safe and think in terms of a 4-year mortgage.

There remained the question of the down payment. If they were to buy a house for $120,000, they would need a 25-per-cent down payment of $30,000 to qualify for a conventional, noninsured first mortgage, plus several thousand dollars more for the legal costs. As things stood, they would only be able to put down about $20,000. That 25-per-cent down-payment rule, however, is not by any means carved in rock, as either a minimum or a maximum.

Several months later, when house prices stabilized – and

in some cases dropped – some of the institutions were asking for 30 or even 35 per cent down, reflecting a certain post-boom nervousness. But at the time John and Judy were looking for money, house prices were still steadily increasing, and that in turn made the bank more friendly. So there was no problem about only having $20,000 as a down payment on a $120,000 piece of property, the bank said: it would grant them a second mortgage of $10,000, at 12 per cent, and also amortized over 25 years. Since this second mortgage would only cost an additional $103.19, that looked like a pretty reasonable proposition to John and Judy, until they sat down and calculated that over 25 years that $10,000 would cost them $20,954 in interest charges. If, on the other hand, they stayed with a single $100,000 mortgage, and placed insurance on it – which the law requires in the case of a high-ratio mortgage – then the house would be 80-per-cent financed. That would call for a one-time 1-1/4-per-cent premium, working out to $1,250 (remembering that it's the whole mortgage that has to be insured), or a monthly payment of $104. In this case, the monthly cost of the second mortgage as compared to the insurance premium would have been almost identical, but had John and Judy borrowed from that bank – in the end, they didn't as we'll see – they would have been far better off going with the single, insured mortgage. That way, they would have escaped some of the burden of amortization, and, within a year or two, they would perhaps have paid down enough of the principal to go back to the bank and demand that the insurance now be taken off.

Either way, with the market so buoyant, they would have no trouble borrowing the $100,000 and for a day or two they were feeling pretty good about things. The next thing they did was contact their lawyer to tell him they were in the market for a house. His fees would be $660, he said, plus whatever the disbursements added up to. "Oh, and keep one thing in mind," he added. "If you put in a offer on a place, make SURE there's a clause attached stating that the deal is conditional on you getting the financing. Otherwise you may lose your deposit."

Armed with this advice, which turned out to be extremely prescient, John and Judy started house-hunting in the $120,000-to-$130,000 range, which was about the rock-bottom level of the Toronto market. And then they had another shock. There was no shortage of houses to look at, but the trouble was, they said later, you wouldn't want to live in most of them. Gone are the days when a Torontonian could buy the traditional "beat-up house on a great street" at a bargain price and fix it up because one of the truisms about a strong property market is that the condition of the house doesn't make a lot of difference to the selling price. In a depressed town, when "For Sale" signs are sprouting like mushrooms on the front lawns, the house that generally DOES get sold is the one that has something special going for it, such as the fact that it's been well renovated, or has a great kitchen (it's amazing in any market how often it's the kitchen that swings the sale). In a hot market, the reverse tends to apply; it's the land that's worth the money, and so location becomes more important than ever.

Although John and Judy eventually profited from that fact, as we'll see, they found themselves in the meantime looking at some dreadful houses with price tags that seemed unreal. When property prices go crazy, there is one school of thought, keenly promoted by the real estate industry, which says that any piece of property is a good buy. In the long term, over a period of 20 years or more, that may be the case, but don't forget that you have to live there in the interim. If you buy a piece of junk, then in the end that's what you've got, and if the reason it's a piece of junk is that it's on a tiny lot, or that there's a factory up the street, or a bus terminal, then there's nothing you can do to change the situation. Wandering from "open house" to "open house," John and Judy found themselves at the bottom end of the market, where most of the pressure was, and they were amazed and disheartened at the way in which run-down, problem-filled houses were snapped up by frantic buyers, often within hours of being listed, and frequently above the asking price. By now, no doubt, there are some people who bought into that overheated market who are wishing they hadn't – particularly people who gambled everything on a short-term mortgage, thinking that house prices could only keep climbing. In the long term, almost all property goes up in value; in the short term, anything can happen.

If you're looking to buy a house, you scour the newspapers, you walk and drive as many miles as you have time for – and you get as many real estate agents as possible working for you because they cost the buyer nothing, ever. (The 5- or 6-per-cent commission, in the event of a sale, is paid entirely by the seller, and, for that reason, a lot of sellers are tempted to dispense with agents altogether, particularly when houses are in demand. Being your own salesman is time-consuming, but on the other hand, in the negotiations for a $150,000 house, not having to pay a commission gives the seller another $9,000 to dicker over.) For buyers, one of the conventions – and fictions – of the business is that a prospective buyer only "goes out" with one agent at a time; nonsense. Be methodical and be ruthless. This is one of the biggest transactions of your life.

John and Judy had at least a dozen agents at work, but

they appeared to be getting nowhere fast because most of the properties in their price range were small, on noisy streets, and a long way from transportation, or had some other drawback. "You know the only way you're going to get a house you like?" said one agent, finally. "You're going to have to get an income property." Click.

So they started playing with some more arithmetic. With a $5 book of amortization tables, they went through various permutations of rental income, interest rates, and amortization periods. Borrowing from the bank at 10 per cent, a monthly rent of $400 from a tenant, before income tax, would service about $45,000 worth of mortgage (a payment of $402.52), if the loan was amortized over 25 years; amortized over 10 years, it would be good for about $30,000 – a payment of $393.11. If the rent was $500, then the figures would be $55,000 ($491.97) and $33,000 ($497.94) respectively. These were only ballpark figures because they didn't take into account property taxes, utility bills, extra insurance costs, maintenance, and all the rest. And income from the apartment would have to be declared, like any other. But theorizing on the basis of a hypothetical basement apartment, John and Judy were able to see the immediate, dramatic effect of this income: it would put within their reach a category of house that would otherwise have been unobtainable.

However, when they went back to the bank to talk things over a second time, they learned that only half the rental income would be taken into account in assessing their worth because income tax would have to be paid on it at the end of the year. John protested that in fact he would probably be able to avoid paying that tax because of other tax credits he had coming, but the bank didn't want to know.

The upshot of this second conversation was that by

scrimping, saving, and bending the bank's rules, and if they could find a house that would produce $500 a month worth of income, the absolute maximum they would be able to afford to spend, including all the expenses of the transaction, was $168,000. Now it just so happened that a few days later – and this is a true story – they found out that they would be getting a $4,000 windfall, and could expect the same amount again, in about 4 or 5 months.

Those were the figures John had in his mind when the phone rang one morning and one of their many real estate agents told them she had a listing for a duplex that had just dropped in price by $20,000 and was available for just under $200,000. Yes, yes, she said, she knew that was more than they could afford, but the point about this property was that it was in one of the most sought-after sections of the city – an area that John and Judy had ruled out. Not only that, but the house had been completely renovated and had a self-contained apartment on the top floor – which was vacant. The agent estimated the apartment could easily be rented out for $700. Before John and Judy went over to inspect the house that night with their agent, they sat down again with their calculator and amortization tables. If they could increase the down payment by $8,000 – borrowing against the windfall – and if they could rent out this supposedly gleaming upstairs apartment for $700, instead of the $500 they'd used in their previous calculations, it might be possible. The extra $200 worth of rent would buy them another $28,000 worth of a 10-per-cent mortgage, amortized over 25 years. The bank would only take half that amount into account, but maybe there was a way round that.

John and Judy took one look at the house and they wanted it. In normal times, anybody who's going to spend $200,000 – on anything – should spend a day or two thinking about it, but these were not normal times. By now, they'd seen enough houses to know that this property looked like a really good deal and would be snapped up. Unfortunately, the fact that something is a good deal has nothing whatsoever to do with one's ability to pay for it – you could be a pauper and find a house for $1 million that's a great deal – and so it was with considerable nervousness that John and Judy went back to the agent's office and wrote out an offer for $197,000. The agent balked a bit when, remembering their lawyer's advice, they stipulated that the offer would have to be conditional on their getting satisfactory financing (a "clean" offer would be more attractive, she said), but they insisted on that, and sealed the deed with a deposit – a cheque for $10,000.

That was just the beginning. The "out" that John and Judy had attached to the offer, the financing condition, would let them off the hook in the event that they couldn't get the bank to play ball. But a conditional offer holds nothing for the seller, who would far rather have a "clean" offer. And in the meantime, there was another buyer hovering in the background, represented by the agent for the seller. Since the commission on the sale is divided between the buying and the selling agent, then in this case the selling agent would get the whole thing, in the event that he sold to his own client. He made it clear to the seller that he didn't think much of John and Judy's offer. In particular, he didn't like the condition.

When the two agents presented their rival offers, the offers were so close that they were "sent back" to the two buyers to be "improved," and, with a mounting sense of alarm, John and Judy found themselves in a bidding war, with the two agents relaying instructions back and forth over the phone. John and Judy increased the offer to just over $200,000, and it was at that point – by now it was past midnight – that the seller introduced a new factor. There was a first mortgage of $145,000 on the house, at 10 7/8 per cent. It had 4 years to run, and he wanted it to be assumed, so as to avoid the 3-month penalty of breaking it, which would cost him in the region of $3,500. The poker game finally ended at 2:00 a.m. when John and Judy agreed to amend their offer and assume the mortgage – and that swung the deal. The new offer was now subject to two conditions, which had to be removed from the offer within 5 days or there was no deal. These were 1) that John and Judy be approved by the lending institution holding the first mortgage, and 2) that they be able to get suitable financing for the balance. In the meantime, they'd got the house.

And then they almost lost it. Monday morning dawned and they went looking for financing. The first priority appeared to be getting a second mortgage. But one thing they failed to realize was that if a person wants to assume a mortgage, he has to apply to the institution in the same way as with any other loan. They'd thought that assuming a mortgage was somehow more of a formality than anything else. What does make things easier, in assuming a mortgage, is the fact that the property itself already has a clean bill of health with the institution, and so is no need for an appraisal, or a survey. But the buyer is not regarded differently from any other borrower. Technically – and a lot of people don't realize this – if a person assumes a mortgage and subsequently defaults on it, then the lending institution CAN hold the original mortgagor responsible. It's rare that this happens because there are a number of other scenarios that get played out first, such as selling the house, but in a market where property values could crash, it's something to note. The bank, however – it bears repeating – is not in the repossession business: it doesn't care what a house could, or could not be worth; it cares about getting its mortgage payment every month.

As John and Judy filled out the forms and talked to the mortgage underwriter, this became clear. Before the institution – one of the major trust companies – would even consider approving them as new mortgagors, it wanted to see proof of employment and salary, proof of the net worth of the apartment, a thorough credit check, and, as well, it wanted some facts about the second mortgage. That second mortgage, which was going to be in the region of $30,000, would have to be at a rate no higher than 12 1/2 per cent, the trust company said.

John and Judy started scrambling. Anyone buying a house is well advised to set aside a couple of days for all the running around. If a second mortgage is required, the business of hunting down the best possible deal can be both complex and full of traps. For that reason, something a borrower has to decide is whether he needs a mortgage broker. A broker's function is much like that of a lawyer in the sense that he gets paid to a) take care of problems, providing a guarantee that what the borrower sees is what he gets, and b) obtain money at the best possible rate. In the case of a straightforward first mortgage, you almost certainly don't need a broker; with a high-ratio second mortgage, a broker may be the only way you can borrow at all.

Either way, it does no harm to phone and ask for a quote on borrowing X amount of dollars. Brokers are conduits for money, and their fees vary widely, generally reflecting the risk – i.e., the financing ratio – inherent in a loan rather than its size. If you want someone to arrange what will be regarded as a high-risk loan, you're going to pay through the nose. The cost of arranging a low-ratio conventional mortgage is as low as $300; large, risky loans can cost thousands of dollars in brokers' fees. Don't hesitate to shop around and say to mortgage brokers: "If you can guarantee me a mortgage of X, at a cost of Y, I'll give you the business." If the market is volatile, the broker may not be able to guarantee the rate in advance because there are too many variables, and he's clearly not going to start phoning around on your behalf until you've agreed to be a client. There's no reason, however, why his fee should not be fixed in advance, in most cases. Brokerage institutes vary considerably, but they aren't allowed to rip you off – they're governed by the same rules that the banking institutions are subject to. The broker will need all the same letters and documentation from you that the bank requires, and with that he'll approach the lenders on your behalf.

And who are those lenders? Institutions, for the most part – banks, trust companies, finance companies – but individuals, as well. A person with $20,000 to invest is not an uncommon figure in the lending world. It's sometimes the case that a private lender will offer a better rate to the borrower than will an institution, but, in general, there's not a huge variance in what's available. The biggest factor will be the financing ratio; in the case of a project that's, say, 50-per-cent financed – i.e., there's a 50-per-cent down payment – a broker might be able to borrow money for his client at perhaps 1/4 or 1/2 of a per cent below the going rate, but that's about all. The newspapers and *The Yellow Pages* are full of mortgage brokers, individuals, and companies with money to lend. But you should beware of anyone who quotes you a great price on a mortgage, particularly a high-ratio one. Make sure there are no concealed fees, such as an inflated appraisal bill, for example. All second mortgagees will want an appraisal, incidentally, so be sure to get a fixed quote in advance on that, too.

After talking to the trust company, John and Judy went to visit a mortgage broker whom their lawyer had recommended. They explained to him that the bank was being "difficult" – that it was insisting that the second mortgage be at no more than 12 1/2 per cent. What were the chances of getting such a mortgage, they asked? Not good, said the broker, because of the financing ratio.

If John and Judy were able to make a $30,000 down payment, the house would still be more than 85-per-cent financed. It was possible that before the closing date – more than 2 months hence – property values would have risen enough that the appraisal (which would in any case have to be done) would permit the second mortgage to be made not on the basis of the selling price of the house, but on its market value. That would alter, marginally, the ratio of the loan, but in the meantime – the broker made a couple of phone calls – the best rate he could offer on the second mortgage was 13 3/4 per cent, amortized over 25 years. However, in order to keep the bank happy, this would be "disguised" as a 12-1/2-per-cent mortgage, and this could be achieved by paying an "up-front" fee of $655, representing the spread between 12 1/2 per cent and 13 3/4 per cent over the term of the mortgage, which would be 2 years.

The broker said he would keep trying to get a better rate than that, but in the meantime he secured a written commitment from a lender, which in this case was a finance company. On top of the "up-front" money, the broker's fee itself had to be paid, which was another $700, while the appraisal would run another $175. The complete cost of arranging the second mortgage thus came to $1,530. In the case of the loan itself, what this boiled down to was that $30,000 was borrowed, but only $29,345 of that was actually received. This was clearly a wonderful deal for the lender – to put out money, immediately get it back, and then get paid interest on it – but it's not uncommon, and neither, in this instance, was it a "dodge." The second mortgage really WAS now at 12 1/2 per cent, because effectively all that had happened was that John and Judy had had to come up with a bigger down payment, so there was no problem as far as the first mortgagee – the trust company – was concerned. But there was, however, another problem: John and Judy's income was insufficient. And so on the Wednesday afternoon, the underwriter for the institution phoned and said no dice. The trust company would not let them assume the mortgage unless they could produce a guarantor – someone to cosign the loan. Meanwhile, the clock was ticking.

There was a relative in the family who – John and Judy were fairly sure – would be willing to cosign the loan and who would be acceptable to the bank. The immediate problem, however, was that their offer on the house was due to expire at midnight, and they were sure that if it did, they would lose the house. The other agent, anxious for a 6-per-cent commission, instead of a 3-per-cent one, still had his client and was probably poised to swoop. There was only one thing to do: they were told by their own agent, who was also starting to sweat, to take off the condition and make a "clean" offer.

If John and Judy had been foolish enough to do this, they could have been in real trouble. As it turned out, the relative willingly cosigned the loan but if, for any reason, he had not, and they had removed the condition, then they would have been stuck. Because, remember, they'd made an offer not just to buy the house, but to assume the

mortgage. If they didn't assume the mortgage – for whatever reason – then they'd have broken the agreement.
And they'd lose their $10,000 – which would go, incident-
ally, not to the seller but to the seller's agent. So what they
did, with some difficulty, was to arrange with the seller for
a 24-hour extension of the condition – in writing – and
that was long enough, just, to get the guarantor okayed by
the trust company. And that did it. No problem now, the
underwriter told John over the phone, the mortgage is
yours; there'll be a $150 fee for the paperwork. But by
now John was feeling nervous, so he went down and got it
in writing – get EVERYTHING in writing. Later that day,
his agent went over to the house with an amended offer,
the conditions removed, and a "Sold" sign appeared on
the lawn.

John and Judy had nearly 2 months, before the closing
date, in which to take stock of their circumstances. The
house had sold for just over $200,000, and of that, the
bulk – about $145,000 – was accounted for by the first
mortgage. The second mortgage provided just under
$30,000, they'd made a $10,000 deposit, and the rest of
the selling price – plus all the costs – they would have to
come up with by the closing date; in all, they estimated –
deliberately using high rather than low figures – they
would need another $20,000. They didn't have that much –
remember they'd only started out with $25,000, and, as
well, they decided they had better have $3,000 left in the
bank, for emergencies – but what they did have coming in
was the extra windfall of $8,000, which they knew they
would have in their hands within 3 or 4 months. So they
borrowed against that money, this time from a friend –
effectively creating a third, if informal mortgage – and
that did it.

There was one other chunk of cash they could get, too:

the rent on the apartment. One of the factors they'd been relying on in all this was the same thing that had forced them to consider buying in the first place: Toronto's acute shortage of good rental accommodation. The apartment was bright, clean, and, like the rest of the house, newly renovated. John and Judy rented it for $725 per month, inclusive, with the tenant to move in at the same time they took possession of the house. One of the differences between paying a mortgage and paying rent is that rent – in this case, first and last month's rent – is payable in advance, whereas a mortgage specifically is not. So that 2 months' rent was another $1,450 they now had use of, and that helped, too.

Their mortgage broker, who had moved swiftly in getting a written commitment for the second mortgage at 13 3/4 per cent, left it to the last week before the closing date to get the house appraised. He reasoned that since prices were still moving up, he might be able to get a better deal on the mortgage if it could be shown that the loan was a smaller percentage of the VALUE of the house than had been originally negotiated. Appraisals of this nature traditionally come in on the low side, reflecting the fact that the appraiser has to cover himself against the eventuality of the borrower defaulting. So everyone (except possibly the seller, had he known) was happy when the figure quoted was $12,000 higher than the selling price. With this new figure, the financing ratio shifted downward to about 82 per cent. But in the meantime, unfortunately, two other things had happened: 1) interest rates had gone up by a percentage point, and 2) a certain nervousness was setting in among some lenders about what was being seen as an overheated market. So in the event, 13 3/4 per cent remained the best the broker could get.

We've mentioned the lawyer's fee, and the broker's fee,

but what about those mysterious legal costs? In Ontario, the biggest item – by far – is the land transfer tax. This tax varies from province to province, and in at least one it doesn't exist at all, which is a big saving. In Ontario, the land transfer tax, always paid by the purchaser, is 1/2 a per cent on the first $55,000 of the purchase, 1 per cent on the balance, up to $250,000, and 1 1/2 per cent over $250,000. In this case, it amounted to a whopping $1,762. On top of that there are usually one or two hundred dollars' worth of costs, which in this case were: obtaining a tax certificate ($10) and a building certificate ($25); paying to register the deed and the mortgage ($16 for each); disbursements ($20.70); xeroxing documents ($9); the cost of certifying cheques ($9) and delivery charges ($36); plus a couple of odds and ends.

A survey wasn't needed, in this instance, because the holder of the first mortgage already had one, and that saved a couple of hundred bucks. Also, there was no default insurance required, in the case of either mortgage. In making the adjustments, John and Judy's lawyer, through whom all the money flowed, explained that there would be two separate payment schedules, one for each mortgage. In the case of the first, the trust company always received its cheque on the first of the month; since the house changed hands halfway through the month, it was arranged that the seller would pay his share of the month's mortgage payment through an adjustment in the final payment made to him, which is usually the way things are done. Likewise, if you get a mortgage from an institution and close the deal on the 20th of January, then even though your first payment may not be until March 1st, remembering that mortgage interest is calculated "not in advance," you are still liable to pay interest on money for the 11 days between January 20th and February 1. In the case of John and Judy's second mortgage, the same "not in advance" clause applied, meaning that their first payment would be made exactly one month after the closing date. In general, this is a plus for the borrower in that he has the use of that money for a month before making his first payment.

All in all, including the cost of paying the "up-front" money for the second mortgage, it cost John and Judy exactly $4,105 for all the costs associated with the purchase of this house costing slightly more than $200,000. That could have been worse, and part of the reason was that both the lawyer and the broker came recommended, and their fees were comparatively low.

That was what it cost them to get the place. But what about the cost of hanging on to it? Here is a breakdown of the monthly budget:

1st mortgage, including property taxes: $1,489.00
2nd mortgage: $320.11
Total: . . . . $1,809.11.

With $725 coming in every month, the figure is reduced to $1,084.11. On top of that is fire/theft/damage insurance, which is about $560 a year, plus all the bills: heat, hydro, water rates, and telephone. The bills are on the low side because the house is well insulated and energy-efficient. Adding everything together, it costs John and Judy about $1,200 a month to own and run their house. They'll have to declare the rent as income, of course, when it's time to do their tax returns, but when they do, they'll have open to them all the options that we discussed in Chapter 3, on income property. We started this chapter by noting that had they rented a decent 2-bedroom apartment, they were probably going to have to spend $1,000, money they would never see again. Instead, by stretching themselves to the limit – and the cost of the house is eating up more than half their disposable income each month, leaving them without a lot of spare cash – they were able to squeeze themselves into the most expensive housing market in Canada.

Only time will show whether they made the right choice, and, indeed, within a few weeks of their making the deal, there were indications of the market, at least in some parts of the city, slowing down. But they had a couple of things going for them. First, as we've noted, if a housing market does slump, perhaps because interest rates take a hike, then the property that's in particularly good condition often becomes the one that will sell. Second, the $8,700 worth of income that their rental unit produces every year – an amount that is unlikely to ever decrease – will also look more and more attractive. And third, by buying a house that as well as requiring no work or repairs is also pleasant to live in, John and Judy have to some extent reduced the danger of getting stuck with something they can't get rid of. (The owner of a very expensive house, incidentally, is also more vulnerable if times get tough and the cost of borrowing becomes prohibitive because the number of potential buyers shrinks.) One of the things they are dependent on is being able to rent out the apartment for a high rent, but another key factor is how long a person wants to live in a house: if he's committed to moving on every year, then he's subject to all the dangers that accompany speculation. But – with some conspicuous exceptions – there are not many houses that are worth less than they were 5 years previously.

We started out by saying a person should buy the biggest house he can because as a tax-free principal residence, there's no better place to invest. We've also noted that if a piece of property increases in value by 10 per cent a year, its worth will double in 7 years. Had John and Judy bought the $120,000 property they had in mind when they began house-hunting, that's how much profit they'd make if they sold it after 7 years. With the $200,000 house, however, not only will they have had a much more pleasant place to live in during that time, but if they sell, they'll be $80,000 better off. And that's tax-free.

Throughout this book, we've talked a great deal about borrowing to buy investments, to buy real estate, to pay off mortgages, and about a range of other footwork. Finally, there's something I really want to emphasize.

Don't, for a second, forget that almost all these moves require professional help, and that if you undertake some of them on your own, you can get into trouble. Where do you go for that help? If you read my last book, *Your Money And How To Keep It*, there's a chapter on finding a financial planner, and that's more relevant than ever: as we've said, financial planning is a growth industry. But do get someone who doesn't exclusively sell his own product. Then there are lawyers, accountants, and real estate agents who can be of help in juggling the numbers. Remember that lawyers and accountants all have their fees, and so do most financial planners, if they're classed as consultants; some, however, are "product-driven," i.e., they get their fees when they invest your money.

And in the end, that's what mortgages are all about: your money.

Index

203

A Note on the Author

Brian Costello is Canada's most trusted financial consultant. Bestselling author of *Your Money and How to Keep It, 101 Year-Round Tax Tips, Step-by-Step Tax Guide, How to Beat the Taxman All Year,* and *Brian Costello's Hometax* (plus a computer program that does your tax return and manages your money year-round), he has a syndicated radio show that is carried daily by as many as 180 stations from coast to coast. As well, Brian appears as financial consultant for several other TV and radio shows throughout Canada. He has a weekly column in 49 newspapers. His articles have appeared in several Canadian publications including *Maclean's, Financial Post Moneywise Magazine, En Route, Toronto Life, Quest,* and *Canadian Business.*